ACADEMIC
ENCOUNTERS
THE NATURAL WORLD

ACADEMIC ENCOUNTERS

The *Academic Encounters* series uses a sustained content approach to teach students the skills they need to be successful in academic courses. There are two books in the series for each content focus: an *Academic Encounters* title and an *Academic Listening Encounters* title. Please consult your catalog or contact your local sales representative for a current list of available titles.

Titles in the *Academic Encounters* series at publication:

Content Focus and Level	Components	*Academic Encounters*	*Academic Listening Encounters*
HUMAN BEHAVIOR High Intermediate to Low Advanced	Student's Book Teacher's Manual Class Audio Cassettes Class Audio CDs	ISBN 978-0-521-47658-4 ISBN 978-0-521-47660-7	ISBN 978-0-521-60620-2 ISBN 978-0-521-57820-2 ISBN 978-0-521-57819-6 ISBN 978-0-521-78357-6
LIFE IN SOCIETY Intermediate to High Intermediate	Student's Book Teacher's Manual Class Audio Cassettes Class Audio CDs	ISBN 978-0-521-66616-9 ISBN 978-0-521-66613-8	ISBN 978-0-521-75483-5 ISBN 978-0-521-75484-2 ISBN 978-0-521-75485-9 ISBN 978-0-521-75486-6
AMERICAN STUDIES Intermediate	Student's Book Teacher's Manual Class Audio CDs	ISBN 978-0-521-67369-3 ISBN 978-0-521-67370-9	ISBN 978-0-521-68432-3 ISBN 978-0-521-68434-7 ISBN 978-0-521-68433-0
THE NATURAL WORLD Low Intermediate	Student's Book Teacher's Manual Class Audio CDs	ISBN 978-0-521-71516-4 ISBN 978-0-521-71517-1	ISBN 978-0-521-71639-0 ISBN 978-0-521-71641-3 ISBN 978-0-521-71640-6

2-Book Sets are available at a discounted price. Each set includes one copy of the Student's Reading Book and one copy of the Student's Listening Book.

Academic Encounters:
Human Behavior 2-Book Set
ISBN 978-0-521-89165-3

Academic Encounters:
Life in Society 2-Book Set
ISBN 978-0-521-54670-6

Academic Encounters:
American Studies 2-Book Set
ISBN 978-0-521-71013-8

Academic Encounters:
The Natural World 2-Book Set
ISBN 978-0-521-72709-9

ACADEMIC ENCOUNTERS

THE NATURAL WORLD

Reading
Study Skills
Writing

Jennifer Wharton

CAMBRIDGE
UNIVERSITY PRESS

CAMBRIDGE UNIVERSITY PRESS
Cambridge, New York, Melbourne, Madrid, Cape Town, Singapore, São Paulo, Delhi, Dubai, Tokyo

Cambridge University Press
32 Avenue of the Americas, New York, NY 10013-2473, USA

www.cambridge.org
Information on this title: www.cambridge.org/9780521715164

First published 2009
2nd printing 2009

Printed in Hong Kong, China, by Golden Cup Printing Company Limited

A catalog record for this book is available from the British Library.

Library of Congress Cataloging-in-Publication Data

Wharton, Jennifer, 1968–
  Academic encounters : the natural world : reading, study skill, writing /
Jennifer Wharton.
     p. cm. -- (Academic encounters)
  "Low Intermediate."
  "The companion book, Academic Listening Encounters: The Natural World,
develops students' listening, note-taking, and discussion skills using
authentic interviews and lectures and a variety of pre- and post-listening
activities."
  ISBN 978-0-521-71516-4 (Student's bk.) -- ISBN 978-0-521-71517-1
(Teacher's Manual)
  1. English language--Textbooks for foreign speakers. 2. English
language--Rhetoric--Problems, exercises etc. 3. Study skills--Problems,
exercises, etc. 4. Earth sciences--Problems, exercises, etc. 5. Readers
(Secondary) I. Title. II. Series.

  PE1128.W57 2009
  428.2'4--dc22

2008052372

ISBN 978-0-521-71516-4 Student's Book
ISBN 978-0-521-71517-1 Teacher's Manual

Art direction, book design, and photo research: Adventure House, NYC
Layout services: Page Designs International, Inc., Fort Lauderdale, Florida

Unit 2 Water on Earth   47

Chapter 3   Earth's Water Supply

Chapter 4   Earth's Oceans

Author's Acknowledgments

In the process of writing this book, I have learned a lot. For one thing, I never knew just how many people it actually takes to produce a textbook. I would like to thank all the people at Cambridge who worked hard to make sure this book happened. First, thanks go to Kathleen O'Reilly, Senior Development Editor, for her support and guidance from the very beginning until the very end. Her talent and experience were always appreciated. Thanks also go to Bernard Seal, Series Editor, for allowing me to take a topic so close to his heart and make it my own; his assistance and insight were invaluable. The contributions of Senior Publishing Manager Janet Aitchison and Senior Commissioning Editor Jane Mairs were much appreciated, as was Lida Baker's willingness to jump in and contribute her ideas. Thanks, too, go to Sylvia Dare, Production Supervisor; Don Williams, Compositor; Robert Litzenberger, Fact Checker; Jill Ginsburg, Copyeditor; and Kellie Petruzzelli, Editorial Assistant. Above all, I am extremely grateful to Amy Cooper, my incomparable development editor. With great skill and encouragement, she helped me navigate more than a few rough patches in bringing this project to its successful conclusion. And somehow she made it look easy.

I am also very grateful to the reviewers of the manuscript who made invaluable comments and suggestions: Nancy Braiman, Byron-Bergen High School; Deborah Gordon, Santa Barbara City College; Susan Lafond, Guilderland High School; Peter Lempert, Hollywood High School; Sarah Lynn, Bridge Program of Harvard University; Kathleen Mahnke, St. Michael's College; Shaun Manning, Hankuk University; and Pelly Shaw, American University of Sharjah.

I would like to thank my colleagues at Transpacific Hawaii College who are some of the finest educators I have had the privilege of working with. Special thanks go to Donna Prather. Her intelligence, sense of humor, and insistence on putting student needs first serve as a model for me each day. Thanks also go to Patty Reiss, Beth Edwards, Jane Spigarelli, and Ann Conable for their ideas and feedback as this book took shape, and to Yoneko Kanaoka, with whom I have been fortunate to share various teaching experiences, professional development projects, and friendship for more than nine years.

Like most teachers, my students have taught me many things over the years. I tried to remember those lessons as I wrote this book.

Finally, I wish to thank my family: my grandmother, father, and sister, whose love and support help keep me sane; my husband, Patrick, and my daughters, Emma and Fiona – who remind me each day of what matters most.

Jennifer Wharton

Introduction

To The Instructor

ABOUT THIS BOOK

Academic Encounters: The Natural World is a reading, study skills, and writing text based on content taught in Earth science and biology courses in high schools, colleges, and universities in the United States.

New features

If you are already familiar with the *Academic Encounters* series, you will discover two new features in *Academic Encounters: The Natural World*:

- **More support for low-intermediate students**
  The book has fewer readings and is one chapter shorter. It has nine, rather than ten, chapters, and each chapter has three, rather than four, readings. This organization allows more space for tasks that support low-intermediate students in accessing the content of the readings and in practicing academic skills.

- **Guided academic writing assignment**
  In addition to tasks in which students answer test questions, complete sentences, and write original sentences, a one-page writing section is presented at the end of each chapter. It provides students with an opportunity to develop their academic writing skills in an assignment related to the content of the chapter or unit. Students are carefully guided through the writing process.

Correlation with standards

Academic Encounters: The Natural World introduces students to topics and skills in U.S. secondary school standards for Earth science and biology. For more information about the standards, go to www.cambridge.org/us/esl/academicencounters

TOEFL® iBT skills

Many of the tasks in *Academic Encounters: The Natural World* (as well as those in all *Academic Encounters* books) teach academic skills tested on the TOEFL® iBT test. For a complete list of the tasks, see the Task Index on page 217.

ABOUT THE *ACADEMIC ENCOUNTERS* SERIES

This content-based series is for students who need to improve their academic skills for further study. The series consists of *Academic Encounters* books that help students improve their reading, study skills, and writing, and *Academic Listening Encounters* books that help students improve their listening, note-taking, and discussion skills. The reading books and listening books are published in pairs, and each pair of books focuses on a subject commonly taught in academic courses.

- Topics in Earth science and biology
  Academic Encounters: The Natural World
  Academic Listening Encounters: The Natural World
- Topics in American history and culture
  Academic Encounters: American Studies
  Academic Listening Encounters: American Studies
- Topics in sociology
  Academic Encounters: Life in Society
  Academic Listening Encounters: Life in Society
- Topics in psychology and human communications
  Academic Encounters: Human Behavior
  Academic Listening Encounters: Human Behavior

A reading book and a listening book that share a content focus may be used independently, or they may be used together to teach a complete four-skills course in English for Academic Purposes.

ACADEMIC ENCOUNTERS READING, STUDY SKILLS, AND WRITING BOOKS

The approach

In the high-intermediate to advanced reading books, students are presented with authentic samples of academic text. The material has been abridged and occasionally reorganized, but on the sentence level, little of the language has been changed. In *Academic Encounters: The Natural World* and *Academic Encounters: American Studies*, authentic materials have been used as the basis for texts that use academic content and style in ways that are accessible to low-intermediate and intermediate students, respectively. In all the Reading, Study Skills, and Writing books, students use the texts to develop their reading and study skills, and the high-interest content of the texts provides stimulus for writing assignments.

The content

The fact that each book in the *Academic Encounters* series has a unified thematic content throughout has several advantages. First, it gives students a realistic sense of studying in an academic course, in which each week's assignments are related to and build on each other. Second, as language and concepts recur, students begin to feel that the readings are getting easier, building their confidence as readers of academic text. Finally, after studying an *Academic Encounters* book, students may feel that they have enough background in the content area to actually take a course in that subject (for example, Earth science or biology) to fulfill part of their general education requirements.

The skills

The main goal of the *Academic Encounters* Reading, Study Skills, and Writing books is to give students the skills and the confidence to approach an academic text, read it efficiently and critically, and take notes that extract the main ideas and key details. But the goal of academic reading is not just to retrieve information. It is also important for a student to be able to display that knowledge in a writing assignment or test-taking situation. For this reason, tasks that develop test-preparation and writing skills appear throughout the books. A longer writing assignment is at the end of each chapter.

The format

Academic Encounters: The Natural World
This book consists of four units, each on a different aspect of the book's content focus. The first three units have two chapters each and the fourth unit has three chapters. Each chapter has three readings of one to two pages.

Academic Encounters: American Studies, Academic Encounters: Life in Society, Academic Encounters: Human Behavior
Each book consists of five units, each based on different aspects of the book's content focus. Units are divided into two chapters, with four readings in each chapter. Readings are one to four pages long.

Preparing to read

Each reading is preceded by a page of prereading tasks called "Preparing to read." Prereading is heavily emphasized since it is regarded as a crucial step in the reading process. Some of the prereading activities introduce students to new vocabulary; others teach students how to get an overall idea of the content. Students also learn to skim for main ideas and to survey the text for headings, graphic material, and terms in boldface, all of which provide important content clues. Other tasks have students think about the topic of the reading, predict its content, and recall their prior knowledge and personal experiences to help them assimilate the new information they are about to encounter in the reading.

After you read

Each reading is followed by a variety of postreading tasks in a section called "After you read." Some tasks ask students to demonstrate their understanding of the text in such ways as answering reading comprehension questions or drawing a graph. Other tasks ask students to reflect on the content to deepen their understanding of it. For example, students may be asked to analyze the structure of the text, looking for main ideas, supporting details, and authorial commentary. Vocabulary tasks require students to learn strategies for comprehending new vocabulary, to demonstrate their understanding of the new vocabulary, to practice using a dictionary, or to update their vocabulary notebooks. In language-focus tasks, students look at some of the salient grammatical features of the text. Students also learn how to highlight a text, take notes, and practice test-taking skills. The rich variety of tasks and task types allows students to experiment with different study-skill strategies and to discover their learning-style preferences.

Writing

There are varied opportunities in the Reading, Study Skills, and Writing books for students to practice their writing skills. Students write original sentences, extended definitions, short papers, essays, text summaries, and journal entries, as well as short answers to test questions. As students continually read and analyze academic English, they begin to acquire insight into its organization and style, and their own writing develops a more academic tone.

Task pages and text pages

Task pages are clearly differentiated from text pages by a colored vertical bar that runs along the outside edge of the page. The text pages have been designed to look like standard textbook pages. The text is in a column that takes up only two-thirds of the page, thus allowing space in the margins for glossed terms and illustrations. Figures, tables, and boxed inserts with additional information are included on text pages, as they are in standard textbooks. This authentic look helps to create a sense for students that they are reading from an academic textbook.

Task commentary boxes and task index

When a task type occurs for the first time in the book, it is headed by a colored commentary box that explains which skill is being practiced and why it is important. When the task type occurs again later in the book, it may be accompanied by another commentary box, as a reminder or to present new information about the skill. At the back of the book, there is an alphabetized index of all the tasks. Page references in boldface indicate tasks that are headed by commentary boxes.

Opportunities for student interaction

To make the book as lively as possible, student interaction has been built into most activities. Thus, although the books focus on reading, study skills, and writing, speaking activities abound. Students discuss the content of the texts; they work collaboratively to solve task problems; they compare answers in pairs or small groups; and sometimes they perform role plays.

Order of units

In terms of reading topics and vocabulary, the order of units is regarded as optimal. In addition, tasks build upon each other so that, for example, a note-taking task later in the book may draw upon information that has been offered in an earlier unit. However, teachers who want to teach the units out of order may do so. They can use the Task Index at the back of the book to see what types of tasks have been presented in earlier units and build information from those tasks into their lessons.

Course length

Each unit of a Reading, Study Skills, and Writing book contains a unit preview section and six to eight readings, and represents approximately 16–24 hours of classroom material, depending on the level of the students. The course can be made shorter or longer. To shorten the course, teachers might choose not to do every task in the book and to assign some tasks and texts as homework, rather than do them in class. To lengthen the course, teachers might choose to supplement the book with content-related material from their own files, to assign Internet research, and to spend more time developing students' writing skills.

To The Student

Welcome to *Academic Encounters: The Natural World*. In this book, you are going to read about themes and ideas in Earth science and biology. The topics in the book have been chosen for their high interest and relevance to life today.

You will also learn the skills you need to be successful in an academic classroom.

You will learn:

- how to read academic texts
- ways to think critically about what you have read
- strategies for dealing with new vocabulary
- note-taking techniques
- methods of preparing for tests
- how to write in an academic style

As you learn and practice these academic skills, you will have many opportunities to discuss the content of the texts with your classmates.

As you continue to read, study, and write about academic texts, your academic reading and writing abilities will improve. After using this book, you may feel that you have enough background information and sufficient academic skills to take a course in Earth science or biology to fulfill part of your general education requirements or just for your own interest. Or, perhaps you will have gained the knowledge and confidence to do so at some future date.

ACADEMIC ENCOUNTERS

THE NATURAL WORLD

Unit 1

Planet Earth

In this unit, we look at the physical features of our planet and the different ways Earth grows and changes. In Chapter 1, we see how Earth is a part of the universe. We also discuss the ways in which our planet is unique, or different from, all the others. In Chapter 2, we focus on various processes that help create and shape our planet.

Previewing the unit

Before reading a unit (or chapter) in a textbook, it is a good idea to preview the contents and think about the topics that will be covered. This will help you understand how the unit is organized and what it is about.

Read the contents page for Unit 1, and do the following activities.

Chapter 1: The Physical Earth

This chapter describes our solar system and the physical features of the planet we live on.

1 How much do you know about our planet Earth? Look at the photographs. Then answer the questions below.

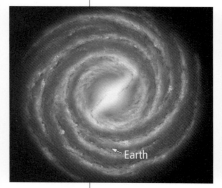  

1 Earth is only one of the planets in the universe, but it is very special. What makes Earth unique, or different from, all the other planets?

2 What makes it possible for people to live on Earth? What does the Earth provide so that we are able to live here?

2 Compare your answers in a small group.

Chapter 2: The Dynamic Earth

This chapter explains that Earth is always moving in different ways. These movements help to form and shape our planet.

Discuss the following questions in a small group:

1 In what ways does Earth move? Have you ever felt it move? If so, describe your experience.

2 The Earth's surface is not flat. There are many landforms, such as mountains and lakes. Name as many other landforms as you can. How do you think these features of Earth's surface formed?

Chapter **1** **The Physical Earth**

Chapter **2** **The Dynamic Earth**

Preparing to read

THINKING ABOUT THE TOPIC BEFORE YOU READ

Thinking about the topic before you read can make the ideas in a text easier to understand.

The text you are going to read discusses some of the objects we see in the sky. How much do you know about these objects? Discuss the following questions in a small group.

1 What are some of the things you see in the sky during the day?
2 What are some of the things you see in the sky at night?
3 Would you like to be a scientist who studies the sky? Why or why not?

PREVIEWING ART IN THE TEXT

Looking at the photographs and illustrations before you read will help you understand some of the ideas in the text.

1 Look at the photograph of our solar system on page 5. Then discuss the following questions with a partner:

1 How many planets are there in the solar system? Do you know any of their names?
2 Can you find our planet, Earth? If you can, draw an arrow (➔) pointing to it.

2 Look at the cartoon on page 6. Discuss the following questions as a class:

1 What do you see in the cartoon? What are they doing?
2 Who is talking?
3 What do you think the main idea of this cartoon is?

Now read

Now read the text "Our Solar System." When you finish, turn to the tasks on page 7.

The Physical Earth

1 OUR SOLAR SYSTEM

Our home in the universe is planet Earth. It is one of eight planets that **orbit**, or circle, the sun. The sun is a star, that is, a giant ball of hot gases. It is the center of our **solar system**. There are billions of other stars in the sky, but the sun is the star closest to Earth. Our solar system also includes moons, which orbit planets. The moon we see in the night sky orbits Earth.

We usually list our solar system's planets in order of their distance from the sun: Mercury, Venus, Earth, Mars, Jupiter, Saturn, Uranus, and Neptune. They can be divided into two groups: terrestrial planets and gas giant planets.

Terrestrial, or Earth-like, planets have solid, rocky surfaces. Mercury, Venus, Earth, and Mars are **terrestrial planets**. Earth is the only planet that has large amounts of liquid water, and it is the only planet that has life. Astronomers (scientists who study the stars and planets) believe that a long time ago, Mars had rivers and oceans just like Earth, but that now all the water is either frozen or underground.

1

orbit
to travel in a circle around a larger object

solar system
the sun and the planets that move around it

2

3

terrestrial planet
a planet with a solid, rocky surface

Gas giant planets are much larger than terrestrial planets. All gas giant planets are made of gases, not solid rock. These planets have rings around them. The rings are made of tiny pieces of rock, dust, or ice. Jupiter, Saturn, Uranus, and Neptune are gas giant planets. Jupiter is the largest planet. It is about a thousand times bigger than Earth.

Outside of our solar system, there are billions of other stars. Astronomers have discovered that some of these stars have planets that orbit them. This means that there are other solar systems in the universe in addition to our own. Perhaps we will even find another planet with life on it someday.

The Story of Pluto

Are there eight or nine planets in our solar system? Before 1930, everyone thought there were eight. Then in 1930, a young man, with no formal training in astronomy, surprised the world. Using a telescope he had made himself, 24-year-old Clyde Tombaugh discovered a new planet in our solar system: Pluto. Pluto is very small, smaller than Earth's moon. It is also farther from the sun than the other planets, so it is colder and darker. After Tombaugh's discovery, people accepted the fact that our solar system had nine planets.

Then, in 2006, the International Astronomical Union (IAU) decided that a planet has to have certain features. For example, it has to make a circular orbit around the sun. It also has to be big enough and strong enough to move away objects in its path. Pluto differs from the other planets in both these ways. First, Pluto has a more irregular orbit. It is not a circle, and it even crosses Neptune's orbit. In addition, Pluto is not strong enough to move objects out of its way as it orbits the sun. For these reasons, the IAU has reclassified Pluto from a planet to a plutoid. So now scientists tell us once again that there are only eight planets.

After you read

Task 1   ASKING AND ANSWERING QUESTIONS ABOUT A TEXT

> Asking and answering questions about a text is a good way to make sure you have understood what you read. You can do it alone or with a partner.

1   Reread paragraph 1 of the text "Our Solar System." Then, with a partner, practice asking and answering questions about what you read. Use the questions below. Add at least one more question to the list.

   1   How many planets are there in our solar system?
   2   What does *orbit* mean?
   3   Is the sun a planet or a star?
   4   (Add your question.)

2   Now reread paragraph 2 of the text. Write two or three questions about the paragraph. Then take turns asking and answering the questions with your partner.

3   Reread the rest of the text and the boxed text "The Story of Pluto." Continue asking and answering questions with your partner.

Task 2   BUILDING VOCABULARY: WORDS FROM LATIN AND GREEK

> Many English words, or parts of words, come from other languages. Words that come from Latin and Greek are especially common in science. Look at these examples:
>
> *terr-* means "earth" or "land"
> *sol-* means "sun"
> *astro-* means "star"
>
> Becoming familiar with word parts from Latin and Greek will help you understand some of the new words you see in science texts.

1   Look back at the text "Our Solar System" and the boxed text "The Story of Pluto," and put a check (✔) above the words that start with *terr-*, *sol-*, or *astro-*.

2   Start a chart of word parts from Latin and Greek in your notebook. Follow this model:

Word part from Latin or Greek	Meaning	English example	Meaning
terr-	*earth, land*	*terrestrial*	*relating to Earth*

Task 3 BUILDING VOCABULARY: CLUES THAT SIGNAL DEFINITIONS

When you read a text with many unfamiliar words, try to understand it without stopping to look up every new word in the dictionary. The definition of a new word is often right there in the text. For example, look at these sentences from the text "Our Solar System":

- It is one of eight planets that **orbit**, or circle, the sun.
- The sun is a **star**, that is, a giant ball of hot gases.
- **Terrestrial**, or Earth-like, planets have solid, rocky surfaces.
- **Astronomers** (scientists who study the stars and planets) believe that a long time ago, Mars had rivers and oceans just like Earth.

Notice how the sentences present the definitions in different ways.

1 Fill in the blanks below with bolded words and phrases from the box. In the first blank for each item, write the word that is defined. In the second blank, write the definition.

1 _____*orbit*_____, or _____*circle*_____, . . .

2 _____, that is, _____.

3 _____, or _____, . . .

4 _____ (_____) . . .

2 Fill in each blank below with an appropriate word from the phrases in step 1.

1 People cannot live on a _____ because it is too hot.

2 _____ use telescopes to learn about the planets in our solar system.

3 The sun does not have a _____ environment.

4 Planets _____ stars, but they do not circle moons.

3 On a separate piece of paper, write three sentences that include definitions of the words below. Use *or*, *that is*, or parentheses in your sentences. Be sure to use correct punctuation.

1 telescope   *A telescope (an instrument that makes faraway objects look larger) is an important tool for an astronomer.*

2 solar system

3 Mercury or Pluto

4 gas giant planet

Task 4 LANGUAGE FOCUS: PARTS OF SPEECH

An understanding of how the parts of speech work in English can help you understand what you read. It can also help you write clear and logical sentences. In this chapter, we review three parts of speech.

A **noun** is a person, place, thing, or idea (*planet, moon, belief*).
A **verb** is an action or a state of being (*orbit, be, have*).
An **adjective** describes a noun or pronoun (*rocky, giant, hot*).

1 Reread paragraph 1 of the text "Our Solar System." Then do the following:

1 Underline all the nouns.

2 Draw two lines under all the verbs.

3 Circle all the adjectives.

Compare your answers with a partner's.

2 Read the paragraph below. Label each noun (*n.*), verb (*v.*), and adjective (*adj.*).

>   *n.* *v.*   *adj.*
>   Mars is an interesting planet. In some ways, it is similar to Earth. It has
>
> weather and seasons. It also has canyons and mountains. However, Mars is a
>
> very different planet from Earth. It is much smaller than Earth, and it is much
>
> colder. In addition, scientists have not found any life on Mars.

3 Read the sentences below. There is a missing word in each one. Decide what part of speech is missing, and write it in the first blank.

_____*verb*_____ **1** Pluto _____ two small moons.

_____ **2** Mercury is a _____ planet.

_____ **3** Saturn has many beautiful _____.

_____ **4** Earth has one _____.

_____ **5** Some people _____ there is life on other planets.

4 Now complete each sentence in step 3 with an appropriate word. Use the part of speech to help you. Compare your sentences with a partner's.

Example: Pluto __*has*__ two small moons.

Task 5 LANGUAGE FOCUS: COMPARATIVE ADJECTIVES

A **comparative adjective** shows the difference between two people, places, or things. Sometimes a comparison includes a group of people, places, or things. Look at these examples:

- Tombaugh was **younger than** most other astronomers when he discovered Pluto.
- Jupiter is **farther** from the sun **than** Earth.
- Saturn's rings are **more beautiful than** Jupiter's rings.
- Venus is **hotter than** the other planets in our solar system.

To form comparative adjectives, follow these guidelines:

> For **one-syllable adjectives**, add *-er*. If the adjective ends in *e*, add only *-r*.
>> small → smaller
>> dark → darker
>> close → closer

> For **one-syllable adjectives that end with a single vowel and a consonant**, double the final consonant and add *-er*.
>> hot → hotter
>> big → bigger
>> red → redder

> For **adjectives with two syllables or more**, add *more* before the adjective. If the adjective ends in *y*, change the *y* to *i* and add *-er*.
>> important → more important
>> solid → more solid
>> happy → happier

> **Irregular adjectives** do not follow patterns. Check your dictionary for a complete list.
>> good → better
>> bad → worse
>> far → farther

To compare two nouns in the same sentence, use *than* after the comparative adjective and before the second noun.

noun 1		comparative adjective		noun 2
Earth	is	smaller	**than**	Jupiter.

1 Find and underline the comparative adjectives in paragraph 4 of the text "Our Solar System" and the boxed text "The Story of Pluto." How many did you find?

2 Write the comparative form of each of these adjectives.

1 dark _____

2 hot _____

3 solid _____

4 icy _____

5 small _____

6 big _____

7 strong _____

8 rocky _____

3 Complete each sentence below with a comparative adjective. Choose from the adjectives in the box, and use each word once. Use correct forms and add *than*. Be sure each sentence is true, based on the information in the texts and the photograph on pages 5–6.

close	cold	~~far~~	hot	large	rocky

1 Uranus is ____*farther*____ from the sun ___*than*___ Mercury.

2 Pluto is _____ _____ Venus.

3 Mars is _____ _____ Pluto.

4 Earth is _____ to the sun _____ Neptune.

5 Mercury is _____ _____ Saturn.

6 Jupiter is _____ _____ Uranus.

4 Compare Jupiter and Pluto. Write three or four sentences, using comparative adjectives and *than*.

Example: *Jupiter is closer to the sun than Pluto.*

1 _____

2 _____

3 _____

4 _____

Preparing to read

PREVIEWING KEY PARTS OF A TEXT

> Previewing key parts of a text before you read it will make it easier to
> understand the main ideas. To preview a text, look carefully at the title,
> the introduction, and the headings. It is also a good idea to read the first
> sentence of each paragraph.

1 Read these key parts of the text "Earth's Four Systems" on pages 13–14:

- the title
- the short introductory paragraph at the beginning of the text
- the headings
- the first sentence of each paragraph

2 Answer the following questions with a partner:

  1 How many systems does Earth have?

  2 What are their names?

3 Now complete the chart below.

  1 Write the names of Earth's systems in the first column of the chart.

  2 Write each of the following key features next to the appropriate system:

   living things • water • Earth's crust and the top layer of the mantle • air

Name of the system	Key feature(s)
lithosphere	*Earth's crust and the top layer of the mantle*

Now read

Now read the text "Earth's Four Systems." When you finish, turn to the tasks on page 15.

2 EARTH'S FOUR SYSTEMS

Think about Earth from the point of view of an astronaut. From outer space, Earth looks like one solid blue ball. In fact, our planet is much more complex. It is actually made up of four very different but interconnected systems: the lithosphere, the hydrosphere, the atmosphere, and the biosphere.

1

The lithosphere
The lithosphere includes Earth's crust and the top layer of the mantle. The **crust** is a thin layer of rock that covers the whole planet. Its thickness ranges from about 5 to 80 kilometers.* The mantle is the section of Earth directly under the crust. The lithosphere is not one solid piece of rock. Instead, it is broken into many smaller pieces called plates.

2

crust
Earth's hard outer layer

The hydrosphere
The hydrosphere is all the water on Earth, including oceans, lakes, rivers, glaciers, rain, and snow. Water covers more than 70 percent of Earth. Approximately 97 percent of Earth's water is salt water from oceans, and 3 percent is freshwater from **glaciers**, lakes, rivers, and groundwater (water under the ground).

3

glacier
a very large amount of ice that moves slowly over land

The atmosphere
The atmosphere is the air surrounding Earth. It is made up mostly of gases. The primary gases are nitrogen and oxygen. Gases in the atmosphere create air for us to breathe, and they protect Earth from the sun's **ultraviolet radiation**. The atmosphere is also where weather conditions, such as clouds and storms, form.

4

ultraviolet radiation
a form of energy that comes from the sun in rays, or lines, that we cannot see

The biosphere
The biosphere is made up of all the living things on Earth. It includes humans, animals, and plants. Life on Earth is very diverse, but all living things share certain features. For example, they all eat, breathe, and grow.

5

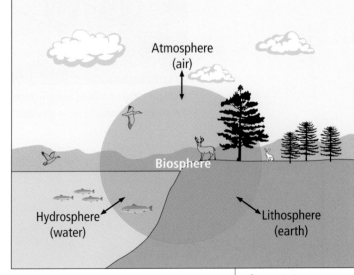

Figure 1.1
Earth's four systems

---

* You can find information about the metric and U.S. systems of measurement on pages 208–209.

The interconnections of Earth's systems

The lithosphere, the hydrosphere, the atmosphere, and the biosphere connect with each other in important ways. We humans are part of the biosphere, but we live on the lithosphere. We depend on the atmosphere for air to breathe and the hydrosphere for water to drink. In fact, these connections are so strong that a change in one system can affect the others. Consider this example: Driving a car contributes to air pollution in the atmosphere. Air pollution causes Earth to grow warmer. Warmer temperatures cause important changes in the hydrosphere: Glaciers melt and ocean levels rise. These changes to the hydrosphere affect the humans, animals, and plants of the biosphere. For example, people who live in coastal areas along the ocean are in danger of losing their homes because of **floods**. The polar bear is gradually losing its **natural habitat** because of warming temperatures in the Arctic. When you think about these interconnections among the systems, it is easy to see that our planet is very complex.

flood
a large amount of water covering an area that is usually dry

natural habitat
the place where an animal or a plant usually lives

Biking instead of driving helps reduce air pollution.
(Of course, it's safer to wear a helmet!)

After you read

Task 1   HIGHLIGHTING

> One way to help you remember what you have read is to highlight
> important information. You can highlight key words and ideas in a text
> by marking them in colors that are easy to see. Remember to highlight
> only the important information. A text that has too many highlighted
> sentences is not useful.

1 | Look back at the text "Earth's Four Systems." Highlight the names of Earth's systems
and the most important feature of each one.

2 | Using a different color, highlight two examples of how Earth's systems interconnect.

3 | Compare your work with a partner's.

Task 2   BUILDING VOCABULARY: WORDS FROM LATIN AND GREEK

> Remember that many words used in science come from Latin or Greek.
> Some of these words have two parts. Knowing the meaning of the
> parts can help you understand the meaning of the word. For example,
> *hemisphere* is made up of *hemi-* (half) and *sphere* (ball). The word
> *hemisphere* means "half of Earth," which is shaped like a ball.

1 | Based on the information in the text "Earth's Four Systems," match the word parts
in the left column with their meanings on the right.

_____ **1** *litho-*   **a** water

_____ **2** *hydro-*   **b** life

_____ **3** *atmo-*   **c** rock, stone

_____ **4** *bio-*   **d** gas, vapor

2 | Circle the correct word in each sentence below.

  1 A spherical cloud is shaped like a (square / circle / diamond).

  2 Lithology is the study of the physical qualities of (rocks / water / gases).

  3 Countries that use hydropower to create energy are using (water / rocks / air).

  4 Atmospherology is the study of (water / rocks / gases).

  5 A biologist works with (rocks / gases / living things).

3 Look back at the sentences in step 2. Circle two examples of the word part *-logy*.

What do you think it means? Write a short definition. _____

Then add *-logy* to your chart of word parts from Latin and Greek.

4 Add the words from the box and step 1 on page 15 to your chart of word parts from Latin and Greek. (Review "Building Vocabulary" on page 7 if necessary.)

Task 3 BUILDING VOCABULARY: LEARNING VERBS WITH THEIR PREPOSITIONS

> Some verbs often occur with specific prepositions, for example: *benefit from, pay for, think about*. When you learn a new verb, notice if a preposition follows. Try to learn the verb and the preposition together as a unit.

1 Each verb in **bold** frequently occurs with a specific preposition. Fill in the blanks with the correct prepositions. If necessary, you can find the verbs in the text "Earth's Four Systems."

1 Its thickness **ranges** _____ about 5 to 80 kilometers.   (par. 2)

2 Gases in the atmosphere create air for us to breathe, and they **protect** Earth _____ the sun's ultraviolet radiation.   (par. 4)

3 The lithosphere, the hydrosphere, the atmosphere, and the biosphere **connect** _____ each other in important ways.   (par. 6)

4 We **depend** _____ the atmosphere for air to breathe and the hydrosphere for water to drink.   (par. 6)

5 Driving a car **contributes** _____ air pollution in the atmosphere.   (par. 6)

2 Complete the sentences below. First, add the correct preposition for each verb in bold. Then select an appropriate ending from the box.

> the sun's dangerous rays   −238°C to −228°C   good health
> ~~other scientists all over the world~~   a cold environment

1 Scientists use the Internet to **connect** *with* *other scientists all over the world* .

2 Sunscreen and sunglasses **protect** people _____ _____.

3 The temperature on Pluto **ranges** _____ _____.

4 Polar bears **depend** _____ _____.

5 Drinking clean water and breathing clean air **contribute** _____ _____.

3 Complete these sentences with something that is true for you.

1 I **depend** _____.

2 The summer temperature where I live **ranges** _____.

3 I want to **contribute** _____.

Task 4 USING A PIE CHART TO ORGANIZE STATISTICS

Textbooks often use statistics, that is, a group of facts stated as numbers. Sometimes it is helpful to organize a group of statistics in a pie chart, which shows the parts of a whole. This makes the statistical information easier to read and understand.

1 Read the following sentence from the text "Earth's Four Systems." Notice how the pie chart on the right organizes the information.

> Water covers more than 70 percent of Earth.

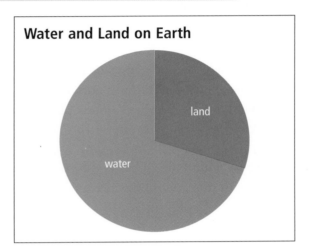

Water and Land on Earth

2 Reread paragraph 3 of the text. On a separate piece of paper, make a pie chart to represent the amount of freshwater and salt water on Earth. Look at your chart and write two sentences about the information. You can start this way:

Approximately _____ percent of water on Earth is freshwater.

3 Work in pairs or small groups. Survey your classmates. You can use one of the questions below or ask your own question about our planet.

- *Do you think there is life beyond Earth?*
- *Which of Earth's four systems are you most interested in learning more about?*

4 Make a pie chart to organize the results of your survey. Give the chart a title and write a few sentences about the information. Be prepared to present your chart and your sentences to the class. You can start your sentences this way:

In our class, _____ percent of the students think . . .

In our class, _____ percent of the students are most interested in . . .

Preparing to read

THINKING ABOUT THE TOPIC BEFORE YOU READ

1 Look at these photographs. Then discuss the questions below in a small group.

a

b

c

1 Do you know the names or locations of any of the places in the photographs?

2 What do they all have in common?

3 What are some other famous places made of rock?

4 What do people use rocks for? Try to think of at least three uses.

5 Did builders use any rocks to construct your school or your home? If so, do you know what kind of rocks they used?

6 What are some things in your school or home that are made of rock?

2 Check your answers to step 1 questions 1–4 at the bottom of the page.

Now read

Now read the text "Rocks on Our Planet." When you finish, turn to the tasks on page 21.

Answers to step 1:
1 a Stonehenge in England, **b** the Great Pyramids in Egypt, **c** Machu Picchu in Peru **2** They are all made of rock. **3** Possible answers: the Taj Mahal in India, the Parthenon in Greece, the Great Wall in China, El Tajin in Mexico **4** Possible answers: building, tools, sculpture, landscaping in gardens

3 ROCKS ON OUR PLANET

Earth is a terrestrial planet, that is, a planet with a rocky surface. It is covered with rocks of all ages. The oldest rocks in Earth's crust are more than three billion years old. The youngest ones are just a few minutes old. All rocks are made of minerals, or inorganic (nonliving) matter.

Although different types of rocks form in different ways, they all come from the same original hot material, **magma**, from deep inside Earth. The three main types of rocks are igneous, sedimentary, and metamorphic.

magma
very hot melted, or liquid, rock that is deep inside Earth

Three main types of rocks

"Igneous" means "relating to fire." When the fiery magma rises up through Earth's crust, it cools and becomes igneous rock. Sometimes the melted rock cools under the surface of the earth, but sometimes magma erupts from a volcano as **lava** and cools on Earth's surface. Granite, basalt, and pumice are examples of igneous rocks.

lava
hot, melted rock that flows from a volcano

Although rocks are very strong, wind and rain over time can break off tiny pieces. These pieces of rock often settle at the bottom of a river or ocean in a layer, and they are called sediment. After thousands of years, more layers of sediment form. The weight from all the layers presses the sediment so tightly together that it eventually becomes solid sedimentary rock. Some common sedimentary rocks are limestone, sandstone, and shale.

The heat and pressure deep inside Earth can actually change one type of rock into another. This process is called metamorphosis, or the process of changing one thing into another. Rocks that form in this way are called metamorphic rocks. For example, when limestone, a sedimentary rock, is under great heat and pressure for a long period of time, it can change into marble, a metamorphic rock.

Figure 1.2
The rock cycle

The rock cycle

Over time, any type of rock can change into any other type. This process is called the rock cycle. Magma cools and forms igneous rocks. Igneous rocks break into small pieces and form sedimentary rocks. Deep inside Earth, great heat

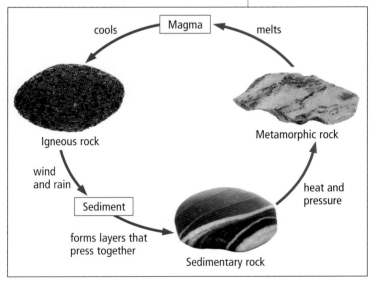

and pressure act on sedimentary and igneous rocks and change them into metamorphic rocks. When all three kinds of rock move even deeper into Earth, they melt, become magma, and the rock cycle begins all over again. In this way, for millions of years, the rocks in Earth's crust have continuously changed form. Rocks are natural recyclers.

Save the Rocks!

There is something very unusual in Narendra Luther's living room – a giant, two billion-year-old rock that goes all the way up through the ceiling to the second floor. This rock is just one of many that formed in Hyderabad, India, billions of years ago. The people in the city have given some of the rocks names, such as Bear's Nose and Stone Heart. Some rocks have become temples, and others have become billboards. A large number have been destroyed to make room for new office buildings, apartments, hotels, and shopping malls. As the city develops, there is less and less room for these giant reminders of Earth's past.

Many people in Hyderabad want to save some of the rocks. The city now has a rock park, and several new buildings include rocks as part of their design, just like Mr. Luther's house. In this way, people can enjoy the new things that come with development, and they can also save part of their past.

The people of Hyderabad hope to save their rocks.

After you read

Task 1   TEST TAKING: ANSWERING MULTIPLE CHOICE QUESTIONS

One common type of question on tests and in textbooks is the multiple choice question. Here are some strategies for answering this type of question:

- Read the question several times. Make sure you understand it before you try to choose an answer.
- Think of the correct answer, and then look for it in the choices.
- Read all the choices before you make a decision. Do not stop reading as soon as you think you have found the correct answer.

Answer the questions below, based on the text "Rocks on Our Planet." Then compare your answers with a partner's.

1 What are all rocks made of?
   a lava
   b water
   c fire
   d minerals

2 Which one of the following is a type of rock?
   a sedimentary
   b organic
   c terrestrial
   d metallic

3 Where do igneous rocks form?
   a on Earth's surface
   b under Earth's surface
   c in a river
   d both on and under Earth's surface

4 Where do many sedimentary rocks form?
   a on Earth's surface
   b under Earth's surface
   c in a river
   d in the wind

5 What forces create metamorphic rocks?
   a wind and rain
   b heat and pressure
   c cooling and melting
   d erupting and breaking

6 Which process causes rocks to change form continuously over time?
   a the formation of sediment
   b the rock cycle
   c volcanic eruptions
   d the cooling of magma

Task 2 LABELING DIAGRAMS

Studying diagrams and labeling them with key words sometimes makes it easier to understand and remember complex information in a text. This strategy is especially helpful when you read science texts.

1 Look at the diagrams below. Find and label these terms: *lava, magma,* and *igneous rock.*

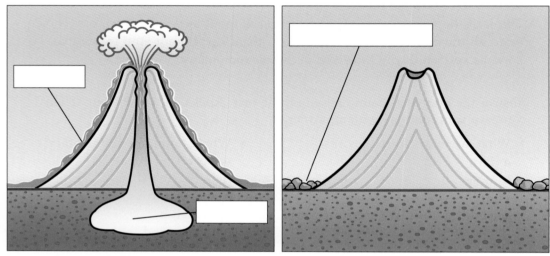

A volcano during and after eruption

2 Look at the diagram of the rock cycle below. Label the blanks with these words: *Metamorphic rock, Sedimentary rock, Igneous rock, Sediment,* and *Magma.*

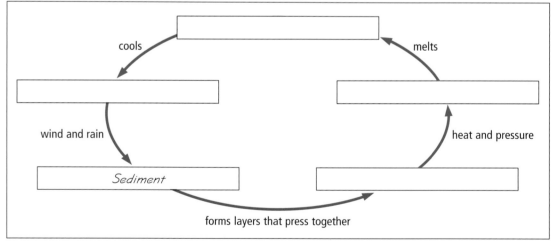

The rock cycle

3 Look back at Figure 1.2 on page 19 to check your work.

Task 3 LANGUAGE FOCUS: SUBJECTS

The **subject** of a sentence names who or what the sentence is about. A sentence in English must have at least one subject. It can be a single noun, a noun phrase (a noun + other words that give more information about the noun), or a pronoun. Pronouns are words that take the place of nouns. The subject pronouns are *I, you, he, she, it, we, they*.

Common mistakes with subjects:

1 There is no subject in the sentence.
    INCORRECT: Discovered a new planet.
  To correct this sentence, add a subject.
    CORRECT: **An astronomer** discovered a new planet.

2 There are two subjects in a sentence without a connector. One of these subjects is often a pronoun. In English, sentences cannot have a double subject.
    INCORRECT: Earth it is a terrestrial planet.
  To correct this sentence, delete one of the subjects.
    CORRECT: **It** is a terrestrial planet.
                 Earth is a terrestrial planet.

1 | Read the following paragraph. The subject of each sentence is underlined.

> The lithosphere includes Earth's crust and the top layer of the mantle. The crust is a thin layer of rock that covers the whole planet. The thickness of the crust ranges from about 5 to 80 kilometers. The mantle is the section of Earth directly under the crust. The lithosphere is not one solid piece of rock. Instead, it is broken into many smaller pieces called plates.

2 | Now read this paragraph and underline the subject of each sentence.

> The atmosphere is the air surrounding Earth. It is made up of gases. The primary gas is nitrogen. The gases in the atmosphere create air for us to breathe. They also protect Earth from the sun's ultraviolet radiation.

3 In the paragraph below, there are three mistakes with subjects. Mark the mistakes and correct them. Then rewrite the paragraph on a separate piece of paper.

Narendra Luther has something very unusual in his house. Is a giant, two billion-year-old stone. This rock is just one of many in the city of Hyderabad, India. The people they in the city have given names to some of the rocks. Have become temples or billboards, but other rocks have been destroyed to make room for new development.

Task 4 LANGUAGE FOCUS: VERBS

Remember that a sentence in English must have at least one subject. It must also have at least one verb. Verbs are words of action (*erupt*, *press*, *move*) or being (*be*, *have*). Sometimes verbs are one word (*erupt*), sometimes they are two words (*is erupting*) or even three words (*has been erupting*).

Common mistakes with verbs:

1 There is no verb in a sentence.
   INCORRECT: Earth terrestrial planet.
   To correct this sentence, add a verb.
   CORRECT: Earth **is** a terrestrial planet.

2 There is only half of a verb. This often happens with the *-ing* form. A verb that ends in *-ing* needs a helping verb.
   INCORRECT: The volcano erupting.
   To correct this sentence, add a helping verb.
   CORRECT: The volcano **is** erupting.
   The volcano **has been** erupting for two days.

1 Reread the first paragraph of the text "Rocks on Our Planet." Underline the subject of each sentence once. Underline the verb twice.

2 Write four sentences about rocks on Earth. Try not to look back at the text. Make sure each sentence has at least one subject and one verb.

3 Exchange your sentences with a partner. Underline the subject of each sentence once. Underline the verb twice. Talk about any problems in the sentences with your partner.

4 Now reread your own sentences. Make any necessary corrections.

Chapter 1   Writing Assignment

Imagine that someone from another planet is coming to visit Earth and that you are the guide. What would you like to tell the visitor about our planet? Write a list of eight to ten sentences with information that you have learned in this chapter about Earth. Follow the steps and the guidelines below.

1 | Have a short conversation with a partner. Talk about the information you would like to share with the visitor. Make a list of your ideas.

2 | Now write the sentences.

> **Guidelines**
> * Include some information about each of the topics you read about: the solar system, Earth's four systems, and rocks.
> * Include some new vocabulary you have learned in this chapter.
> * Be sure that each sentence has a subject and a verb (see the Language Focus tasks, pages 23–24).
> * Try to include some comparative adjectives (see the Language Focus task, page 10).
> * Use subject pronouns correctly (see the Language Focus task, page 23).

3 | When you finish, exchange sentences with a partner and read each other's work. Put a check (✔) next to your partner's three best sentences.

4 | Discuss the following questions about both sets of sentences:

  1 Explain why you picked the sentences you did.

  2 Compare your sentences with your partner's. Did you choose similar information to tell the visitor, or did you choose different things to say?

  3 Look at the structure of the sentences. Do they all have a subject and a verb? Find and underline the subjects in your partner's sentences. Draw two lines under the verbs.

  4 Are there any adjectives in the sentences? If so, what do they describe? Circle the adjectives. Find and label any comparative adjectives (*CA*).

5 | Make any changes that you think would improve your sentences and rewrite them.

Preparing to read

BUILDING VOCABULARY: PREVIEWING KEY WORDS

> Learning the meaning of key words before you read will introduce you to important ideas in a text and make the text easier to understand.

1 Read the following sentences and think about the meanings of the words in **bold**. Use all the words in each sentence to help you.

_e_ **1** Earth has seven **continents**. Asia is the largest continent, and Australia is the smallest.

_____ **2** The Pacific Ocean surrounds (goes all around) the **islands** of Hawaii.

_____ **3** The Pyrenees are mountains that form a **boundary** between France and Spain.

_____ **4** The Mid-Atlantic **Ridge** in the Atlantic Ocean is the longest mountain range on Earth.

_____ **5** The ocean floor is not flat. It has many tall ridges and deep **trenches**. For example, in the Pacific Ocean, the Mariana Trench is almost 11,000 meters below the surface of the ocean.

_____ **6** Earth's crust is not solid. It is made up of many different **plates**.

2 Match the following definitions with the words in **bold** in step 1 above. Write the letter of the definition next to the appropriate sentence.

a a line that divides two places or areas

b large pieces of Earth's crust

c a chain of mountains

d areas of land completely surrounded by water

e very large areas of land, often made up of many countries

f long, narrow, deep holes

Now read

Now read the text "Plate Tectonics." When you finish, turn to the tasks on page 29.

The Dynamic Earth

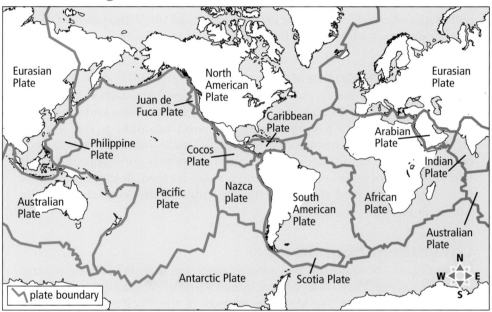

Eurasian Plate

North American Plate

Juan de Fuca Plate

Caribbean Plate

Eurasian Plate

Arabian Plate

Philippine Plate

Cocos Plate

Indian Plate

Australian Plate

Pacific Plate

Nazca plate

South American Plate

African Plate

Australian Plate

Antarctic Plate

Scotia Plate

N
W • E
S

plate boundary

1 PLATE TECTONICS

Earth is always moving. You may not feel it, but our whole planet is turning as it orbits the sun. There are movements on Earth's surface, too. For example, each year South America moves approximately two centimeters farther away from Africa, the islands of Hawaii move about seven centimeters to the northwest, and Mount Everest slowly rises five millimeters upward. Why are continents, islands, and mountains moving? For many years, scientists did not have an answer.

If you look at a map of the world, you may notice that the continents seem to fit together like pieces of a puzzle. In 1912, the German scientist Alfred Wegener suggested that millions of years ago, Earth had just one giant continent. He called it Pangaea ('pan-GEE-uh'), which means "all the Earth" in Greek. Wegener believed that over time, Pangaea broke apart, and the pieces drifted, or moved, to where the continents

1

2

are today. He called his idea **continental drift theory**, but this idea did not explain how the continents moved. He didn't know what scientists know today. They have discovered the reason for the movement: It is called **plate tectonics**.

Tectonic plates and plate boundaries

In the 1960s, scientists discovered that Earth's crust is broken into large pieces called tectonic plates. Although the exact number of plates is not clear, many scientists agree that there are about 12 large plates and several smaller ones. These plates are under the continents (continental plates) and under the oceans (oceanic plates). The plates, and the continents and oceans on top of them, move in different directions and at different speeds over Earth's surface. Tectonic plates interact at places called plate boundaries. There are three types of plate boundaries: divergent boundaries, convergent boundaries, and transform boundaries. 3

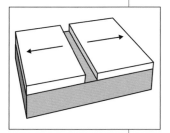

Divergent plate boundary

Divergent boundaries

At divergent boundaries, two plates move away from each other. When two oceanic plates diverge, the ocean floor spreads out and an underwater ridge (mountain range) forms. A good example is the Atlantic Ocean. Millions of years ago, the Atlantic Ocean was a very small body of water. As the plates under it diverged, the ocean grew approximately two centimeters wider each year, and a ridge formed. Today the Atlantic is a huge ocean, and the Mid-Atlantic Ridge is the longest mountain range on Earth. 4

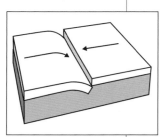

Convergent plate boundary

Convergent boundaries

At convergent boundaries, two plates come together. When two oceanic plates converge, they form a trench and a group of islands, such as the Mariana Trench and the Mariana Islands in the Pacific Ocean. When an oceanic and a continental plate converge, they create a trench and a mountain range. The Peru-Chile Trench and the Andes Mountains formed in this way. When two continental plates converge, a mountain range forms. This process created the Himalayas, the great mountain range in Asia. 5

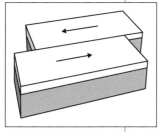

Transform plate boundary

Transform boundaries

At transform boundaries, two plates slide past each other. As they move, they can bump, or hit each other. This movement often causes an earthquake, which is a movement of Earth's crust. People who live along the coast of California often experience earthquakes. They are very common at the transform boundary between the Pacific Plate and the North American Plate. 6

Continental drift has not stopped. Even though the plates move just a few centimeters a year, over a long period of time, they cause Earth to grow and change in dramatic ways. 7

After you read

Task 1 USING HEADINGS TO REMEMBER MAIN IDEAS

After you read a text, you can look back at the headings and use them to help you remember the main ideas.

1 Read these headings from the text "Plate Tectonics."

a Tectonic plates and plate boundaries **c** Convergent boundaries

b Divergent boundaries **d** Transform boundaries

2 Work with a partner. Match the headings in step 1 with the main ideas below. Write the letter of the heading next to the appropriate sentence.

_____ **1** Sometimes two plates move away from each other. This often creates ridges.

_____ **2** Sometimes two plates come together, creating mountains, islands, and trenches.

_____ **3** Earth's crust is divided into about 12 large pieces and several smaller ones that move and interact with each other.

_____ **4** When two plates slide by each other, they can bump. This often causes an earthquake.

Task 2 BUILDING VOCABULARY: PREFIXES

A **prefix** is a word part that comes at the beginning of a word. Each prefix has a meaning. For example, the prefix *re-* means "again" in words such as *reread* and *rewrite*. If you reread a book, you read it again, and if you rewrite a letter, you write it again. Knowing the meaning of a prefix can often help you guess the meaning of a word.

Prefix	Meaning
con-	together, with
cent-	one hundred
inter-	between two or more things or groups
mil-	one thousand

1 Work with a partner. Find and circle the following words in the text "Plate Tectonics": *centimeters, millimeters, converge, interact*. Then use the prefixes to guess the meanings of the words. Use a dictionary if necessary.

2 Here are some new words with the prefixes you learned:

century	convention	interplanetary	millennium

Fill in the blanks in the following sentences with the correct words from the box.

1 Do you think that someday there will be _____ flights between Earth and Mars?

2 The most powerful earthquake of the past _____ happened in Chile in 1960. It was the strongest earthquake in the last 100 years.

3 This week, there is a _____ of astronomers at the university. Hundreds of astronomers are meeting to talk together about their research.

4 Many people had parties to celebrate the start of the new _____ in the year 2000.

3 What other words start with the prefixes *cent-*, *con-*, *inter-*, or *mil-*? Make a class list.

Task 3 LANGUAGE FOCUS: PREPOSITIONAL PHRASES

> A **prepositional phrase** consists of a preposition + a noun (or noun phrase) or a pronoun. Examples are: *on Earth's surface*, *in the 1960s*, and *at different speeds*.
>
> preposition   noun phrase
> Example: **on   Earth's surface**
>
> Prepositional phrases often answer the questions *Where?*, *When?*, or *How?*

1 In the text "Plate Tectonics," find and underline the prepositional phrases below. Then write *Where?*, *When?*, or *How?* in the blanks to show which question each phrase answers.

Where? **1** on Earth's surface   _____ **4** under the continents

_____ **2** along the coast of California   _____ **5** at different speeds

_____ **3** (millions) of years ago   _____ **6** in this way

2 Work with a partner. Find and underline six more prepositional phrases in the text. Decide if each phrase answers the question *Where?*, *When?*, *How?* or none of these.

Task 4 READING MAPS

> Maps show different places on Earth's surface. They can help you find the places you read about. Most maps have a key that includes information to help you read them. In addition, they usually have a compass or a drawing that shows the directions: North, South, East, and West.

1 Look at the map of the world's tectonic plates on page 27. Work with a partner and find these continents: Eurasia (Europe and Asia), North America, South America, Antarctica, Australia, Africa.

2 Based on the information on the map, write *T* (true) or *F* (false) in the blank before each sentence.

_____ **1** The North American Plate is northeast of the Pacific Plate.
_____ **2** The Pacific Plate is smaller than the African Plate.
_____ **3** The Nazca Plate is east of the South American Plate.
_____ **4** The Australian Plate is south of the Indian Plate and the Philippine Plate.
_____ **5** There is no Atlantic Plate.

3 Write three more sentences about the map. They may be either true or false. Exchange sentences with a partner. Decide if your partner's sentences are true or false.

Task 5 WRITING SIMPLE AND COMPOUND SENTENCES

You have learned that every English sentence must have at least one subject and one verb. A sentence with only one subject and one verb is called a simple sentence.

subject   verb
Continental drift   **continues**   today.

A sentence with more than one subject, more than one verb, and a coordinating conjunction (connecting word) is called a compound sentence. The most common coordinating conjunctions are *and*, *or*, **and** *but*. **There is always a comma before these conjunctions.**

                              coordinating
subject   verb   conjunction   subject   verb
Some plates are under the continents,   and   some plates are under the oceans.

Try to use both simple and compound sentences in your writing. Varying the sentence structure will make your writing more interesting to read.

1 Look back at the text. Find three examples of simple sentences and three examples of compound sentences. Write the sentences on a separate piece of paper. Underline all the subjects once and the verbs twice. Circle any coordinating conjunctions. Compare your answers with a partner's.

2 Write four or five sentences about what you learned in the text "Plate Tectonics." Try not to look back at the text. Include both simple and compound sentences. Some words you can use are *continental drift theory*, *continents*, *Pangaea*, *tectonic plates*, *divergent boundaries*, *convergent boundaries*, and *transform boundaries*. Compare your sentences in a small group.

Preparing to read

BUILDING BACKGROUND KNOWLEDGE ABOUT THE TOPIC

> Learning some basic facts about the topic of a text before you read can help you understand the text more easily.

1 | Read the following paragraph about volcanoes.

A volcano is a mountain with a hole at the top. When a volcano erupts, it throws smoke, gas, and lava (melted rock) out of the hole. Some volcanoes, like Mauna Loa in Hawaii, are active. This means that they are erupting, or they could erupt at any time. Other volcanoes are extinct, or dead. Scientists believe these volcanoes will not erupt again.

2 | Discuss the following questions with a partner:

1 Are there any volcanoes where you live? Are they active or extinct?

2 Do you know the names of any famous volcanoes? If so, which ones?

3 Have you ever seen a volcano erupt? If so, where did you see it? What did you see?

Now read

Now read the text "Volcanoes." When you finish, turn to the tasks on page 35.

2 VOLCANOES

One afternoon in 1943, a farmer in Paricutín, Mexico, went to his corn-field, where he saw something unusual. It was a hole in the ground with smoke coming out of it. The next day, there was a 10-meter hill in the same place. Rocks were flying from the hilltop, and lava was flowing down its sides. After one year, the hill was 450 meters high and it continued to erupt. The farmer was amazed and frightened, too. He had observed the birth of a volcano.

1

The formation of volcanoes

When the magma under Earth's crust breaks through to the surface, it creates a volcano. Volcanoes usually form at plate boundaries, where the crust is the weakest. More than 75 percent of Earth's volcanoes are located around the Pacific Plate, in a region called the Ring of Fire. In the Atlantic Ocean, there are many volcanoes at the boundary between the North American Plate and the Eurasian Plate. Directly on top of the two diverging plates is the volcanic island of Iceland.

2

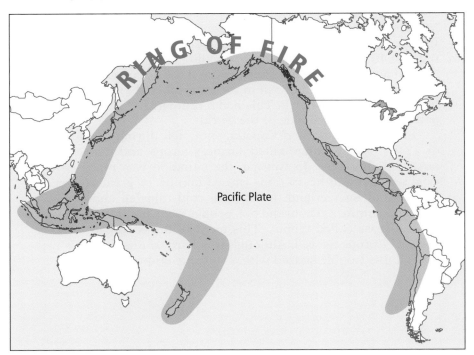

Figure 2.1
The Ring of Fire

Most volcanoes form near plate boundaries, but a few do not. Instead, they form in the middle of a plate over a hotspot, a hole in Earth's crust that allows magma to flow through it. The lava from the hotspot eventually creates a volcanic island. As the plate continues to move over the hotspot, a new volcanic island forms nearby. Over millions of years, this process results in a whole chain of islands. This is how the Hawaiian Islands were formed.

3

Active and extinct volcanoes

4

In the world today, there are approximately 1,500 active volcanoes. Scientists consider a volcano active if it is erupting or if it could erupt sometime in the future. Active volcanoes can be extremely destructive. Lava, gases, **ash**, and rocks can suddenly erupt from a volcano, destroying everything around it. One active volcano is Mount Vesuvius, which erupted in 79 CE and buried the city of Pompeii, Italy, in ash. Other major destructive volcanic eruptions on our planet have been: Mount Tambora (Indonesia, 1815), Mount Krakatau (Indonesia, 1883), and Mount Pelée (Martinique, 1902).

Some volcanoes will not erupt again. These are called extinct volcanoes. Scientists generally agree that Hawaii's oldest volcano, Kohala, is extinct.

5

Although it is clear that volcanoes can be destructive and deadly, they can also have a positive effect on Earth. Volcanoes form new mountains, new islands, and new land. In this way, volcanic activity is an important natural process that contributes to our planet's growth.

6

ash

the soft gray or black powder that is left when something burns

The Year Without a Summer

Many scientists believe that the eruption of Mount Tambora in Indonesia in 1815 was the most destructive volcanic eruption in the past 10,000 years. When the volcano finally stopped erupting, more than 30 centimeters of ash covered the ocean. Over the next year, the large amount of ash in the atmosphere blocked the sun's rays from reaching Earth. This had a dramatic effect on weather patterns on the other side of the world.

In New England and Canada, snow fell during the summer of 1816. Cold weather killed farmers' crops and caused serious food shortages. In Europe, the situation was much worse. Cold weather and heavy rains caused famine, or great hunger, in France and Switzerland. In Ireland, cold rain fell almost every day that summer. Thousands of people went hungry, and many got a disease called typhus. This terrible illness spread to other parts of Europe as well. Although it is hard to imagine, it is true that all this trouble started with a volcanic eruption.

After you read

Task 1   TEST TAKING: ANSWERING TRUE/FALSE QUESTIONS

> True/false questions are common on tests and in textbooks. Here are
> some guidelines for answering this type of question:
>
> - Most activities and tests with true/false questions have approximately
>   the same number of true sentences and false sentences.
> - Sentences with words like *never*, *always*, *only*, and *all* are often false.
> - Sentences with words like *often*, *many*, and *sometimes* are often true.

1   Based on the information in the text "Volcanoes," write *T* (true) or *F* (false) in the
blank before each of the following sentences.

   _____ **1** Volcanoes often form at places where Earth's crust is weak.   par. _____

   _____ **2** The Ring of Fire is in the Atlantic Ocean.   par. _____

   _____ **3** Iceland is directly on top of two divergent plates.   par. _____

   _____ **4** Hotspots are not located near plate boundaries.   par. _____

   _____ **5** One giant volcanic eruption formed the Hawaiian Islands.   par. _____

   _____ **6** Today the world has approximately 15,000 active volcanoes.   par. _____

   _____ **7** Mount Vesuvius in Italy is an active volcano.   par. _____

   _____ **8** Volcanoes always have a negative effect on Earth.   par. _____

2   After each sentence in step 1, write the number of the paragraph in the text where
you found the information.

3   Work with a partner. Find the sentences you marked false in step 1 and correct them.

Task 2   BUILDING VOCABULARY: WRITING DEFINITIONS

> Writing the definition of a word helps you remember it. Here are two
> common ways to write a definition:
>
> (A) _____ **is a** _____.
>   A plate **is a** large piece of Earth's crust.
>   Marble **is a** metamorphic rock.
>
> (A) _____ **is a** _____ **that** . . .
>   A planet **is a** large object **that** orbits the sun.

1 Complete the definitions of the words in **bold** below. Base your answers on what you learned in the text "Volcanoes." Try not to look back at the text.

   1 A **hotspot** is a _____.

   2 An **active volcano** is a volcano that _____.

2 Complete the definitions of the words in **bold** below. Base your answers on what you learned in Text 1, "Plate Tectonics." Try not to look back at the text.

   1 **Tectonic plates** are _____.

   2 A **ridge** is _____.

   3 An **earthquake** is a _____.

3 Compare your definitions in steps 1 and 2 with a partner's. Look back at the texts to check your work.

Task 3 READING BOXED TEXTS

Many academic textbooks include boxed texts. They usually contain interesting material that will add to your understanding of the main text.

Boxed texts can have different purposes. For example, they may:

- give interesting examples of ideas in the main text
- give more details about a topic in the main reading
- discuss a topic that is closely related to the topic of the main text
- help you apply the information from a text to your own life
- present a point of view, or way of thinking about something, that is different from the one in the main text

1 Reread the boxed text "The Year Without a Summer" on page 34.

2 In a small group, discuss the purpose of the boxed text. Does it match any of the purposes in the box above?

3 Look back at the boxed texts in Chapter 1 on pages 6 and 20. What is the purpose of each boxed text? Write your answers below.

- "The Story of Pluto": _____
- "Save the Rocks!": _____

Task 4 USING CORRECT PARAGRAPH FORM

A **paragraph** is a group of sentences about the same topic. In general, paragraphs in English have five to seven sentences, but they can be shorter or longer. When you write a paragraph, follow these rules of form:

- Indent the first sentence of a paragraph. That means, start the first sentence five spaces from the left margin. Sometimes you will see paragraphs that do not follow this rule. However, in your writing, you should always indent the first sentence.
- Begin each sentence with a capital letter and end it with a period, a question mark, or an exclamation point.
- Write one sentence directly after another sentence until you get to the end of a line. Be sure not to use a separate line for each sentence.

1 Look at the following paragraph. With a partner, identify three ways this paragraph uses correct form.

>   If you look at a map of the world, you may notice that the continents seem to fit together like pieces of a puzzle. In 1912, the German scientist Alfred Wegener suggested that millions of years ago, Earth had just one giant continent. He called it Pangaea, which means "all the Earth" in Greek.

2 The following text does not follow the rules of correct paragraph form. Rewrite it as a paragraph on a separate piece of paper. Use correct form and correct punctuation.

> There are four basic types of volcanoes: shield volcanoes, composite volcanoes, cinder cone volcanoes, and supervolcanoes.
> shield volcanoes are generally very large, and lava usually flows down their sides.
> Composite volcanoes are smaller than shield volcanoes.
> They can have both small eruptions and big eruptions
> The smallest type of volcano is the cinder cone volcano.
> For example, the Paricutín volcano was a cinder cone volcano.
> the largest and most dangerous volcanoes are supervolcanoes, and they can cause a lot of destruction.
> Scientists continue to study these four types of volcanoes to learn more about our planet.

3 Compare the paragraph you wrote with a partner's.

Preparing to read

1 Work with a partner. Look at the photograph and answer the questions below.

   1 What do you see in the photograph?

   2 What do you think happened?

   3 Where and when do you think the photo was taken?

2 Discuss the following questions in a small group:

   1 What is an earthquake?

   2 Why do some places, such as California and Japan, have so many earthquakes?

   3 Does the place where you live have earthquakes?

   4 Have you ever been in an earthquake? If so, describe your experience.

   5 What are three things people can do to stay safe during an earthquake?

Now read

Now read the text "Earthquakes." When you finish, turn to the tasks on page 41.

3 EARTHQUAKES

As 1974 came to an end and the new year began, animals in Haicheng, China, started acting strangely. Snakes normally hibernate underground during the winter, but they suddenly came out of their holes. Dogs began to bark and run around wildly, and horses became so upset that some ran away. Why were the animals acting like this? Many people think that the animals sensed what was coming: On February 4, 1975, the earth began to shake, and most of the buildings collapsed. A very large earthquake had struck the city of Haicheng.

1

What causes earthquakes?

When the tectonic plates that make up Earth's crust move past each other, they often bump or rub against each other. The earth above the plates moves as well. This movement is called an earthquake. Sometimes the plates get stuck. The pressure increases as the two plates try to move past each other but cannot. They finally move with a sudden and powerful jerk, which can also cause an earthquake. During a small earthquake, the earth simply shakes a little, and people may not even notice. However, a strong movement can cause the earth to shake and roll violently. It can make buildings and bridges fall. It can also cause the earth to split open and form a large **fault**, or crack.

2

fault
a large break in the surface of the earth

Where do earthquakes happen?

Earthquakes can happen anywhere, but certain places have more earthquakes because they sit on tectonic plates that move frequently. One example is the area around the Pacific Plate, which includes China, the Philippines, Japan, and the western coasts of Canada, the United States, and South America. Earthquakes are common in those places. The deadliest earthquake in modern times happened in 1976 in Tangshan, China. It lasted less than two minutes, but more than 250,000 people died, and more than 90 percent of the buildings collapsed. Earthquake scientists study places like Tangshan because of the many faults in these areas and the activity of the tectonic plates.

3

San Andreas fault in California

Can people prepare for an earthquake?

Scientists are not able to predict when an earthquake will happen. However, they can identify the areas where earthquakes are most likely

4

to occur. This information can help people in those areas prepare. They can learn what to do before, during, and after an earthquake. Engineers in those areas can build bridges and buildings that are better able to survive earthquakes. We cannot stop tectonic plates from moving, but with accurate information and good planning, we can help people live more safely on our planet.

Could Los Angeles fall into the ocean?

California is famous for its earthquakes, such as the one that almost destroyed the city of San Francisco in 1906. Many people believe that part of California could even break off and fall into the Pacific Ocean during an earthquake. Why do many people have this idea?

California is the meeting place of two tectonic plates. Most of the state is on the North American Plate. The southwestern part of the state (including Los Angeles) is on the Pacific Plate. The two plates meet at a transform boundary called the San Andreas fault. From the air, the fault looks like a line that neatly separates the western and eastern parts of the state. It is easy to imagine these two sides tearing apart, or away, from each other in a large earthquake. This cannot happen, though, because the two plates are actually sliding past each other, not away from each other. In fact, the Pacific Plate is moving in a northwest direction at the rate of about 46 millimeters per year. Since Los Angeles is on the Pacific Plate and San Francisco is on the North American plate, millions of years from now, the two cities will be neighbors. It is also true that Los Angeles will never fall into the ocean because the southwestern part of California and the Pacific Ocean are on the same plate.

After you read

Task 1 READING FOR MAIN IDEAS

> It is very important to learn how to find the main idea of a paragraph or longer text. This skill will help you understand what you read. To identify the main idea of a text, ask "What is it about?" or "What idea do all the sentences discuss?"

1 Look back at the text "Earthquakes." Write the number of the paragraph that discusses each of the following main ideas.

    1 Some places experience more earthquakes than others.   par. _____

    2 Animals may have predicted an earthquake that struck Haicheng, China, in February of 1975.   par. _____

    3 Earthquakes happen when two tectonic plates bump or get stuck as they move past each other.   par. _____

    4 Scientists cannot predict when an earthquake will happen, but their information can help people prepare.   par. _____

2 Check (✔) the sentence below that expresses the main idea of the whole text.

_____ **1** A serious earthquake occurred in Haicheng, China, in 1975.

_____ **2** Earthquakes, caused by the movement of tectonic plates, can happen anywhere, and people need to prepare for them.

_____ **3** It is impossible to prepare for earthquakes because no one knows when they will happen.

_____ **4** Earthquakes usually last a very short period of time, but they can kill thousands of people and cause buildings to collapse.

Earthquake damage in Taiwan, 1999

Task 2 BUILDING VOCABULARY: USING GRAMMAR AND CONTEXT TO GUESS NEW WORDS

Sometimes you can use grammar and context to guess the meaning of new words.

Grammar: Look at the part of speech. It tells you if the new word is a thing (noun), an action (verb), or a descriptive word (adjective).

Context: Look at the words and sentences before and after a new word. They often include a definition or a description that can help you guess the meaning.

Tip: Your background knowledge can also help you.

1 │ Read the following paragraph from the text "Earthquakes."

> As 1974 came to an end and the new year began, animals in Haicheng, China, started acting strangely. Snakes normally **hibernate** underground during the winter, but they suddenly came out of their holes. Dogs began to **bark** and run around wildly, and horses became so **upset** that some ran away. Why were the animals acting like this? Many people think that the animals **sensed** what was coming: On February 4, 1975, the earth began to shake and most of the buildings **collapsed**. A very large earthquake had struck the city of Haicheng.

2 │ Work with a partner. Match the words in **bold** in step 1 with the definitions below. Use the strategies in the box at the top of the page.

Example: Snakes normally **hibernate** underground during the winter.

Strategies
- grammar: You can guess that the word *hibernate* is a verb (an action).
- context: The other words in the sentence tell you that *hibernate* is something that animals do underground during the winter.

- background
  knowledge: You may know that some animals sleep during the winter.

hibernate	**a** sleep during the winter
_____	**b** felt something without seeing or hearing it
_____	**c** make a loud animal noise
_____	**d** fell down
_____	**e** worried, unhappy

3 │ Discuss your answers in a small group. Tell which strategies you used to guess each word.

Task 3 LANGUAGE FOCUS: UNDERSTANDING PRONOUN REFERENCE

Pronouns are words that take the place of nouns in a sentence. Writers use pronouns to avoid repeating the same nouns again and again. To understand the meaning of a pronoun, you need to find the noun it refers to. The following guidelines will help you:

- Look for the noun that comes before the pronoun. A pronoun usually refers back to a noun that has been mentioned recently.
- Notice if the pronoun is singular or plural. That will tell you if you are looking for a singular or a plural noun.

1 | Read the sentences below from the text "Earthquakes." The pronouns are underlined. Draw an arrow from each pronoun to the noun or noun phrase it refers to.

1 When [the tectonic plates] that make up Earth's crust move past each other, they often bump or rub against each other.

2 The pressure increases as the two plates try to move past each other but cannot. They finally move with a sudden and powerful jerk.

3 However, a strong movement can cause the earth to shake and roll violently. It can make buildings and bridges fall. It can also cause the earth to split open and form a large fault, or crack.

4 The deadliest earthquake in modern times happened in 1976 in Tangshan, China. It lasted less than two minutes, but more than 250,000 people died, and more than 90 percent of the buildings collapsed.

5 Scientists are not able to predict when an earthquake will happen. However, they can identify the areas where earthquakes are most likely to occur.

2 | Compare your work with a partner's.

Task 4 LANGUAGE FOCUS: SHOWING CONTRAST WITH *BUT* AND *HOWEVER*

> Writers can contrast (show the difference between) ideas by using words like *however* and *but*.
>
> The word *however* often starts a sentence. There is always a comma after it.
>
> • An active volcano may not have erupted in thousands of years. **However**, it could erupt sometime in the future.
>
> The word *but* comes in the middle of a sentence and has a comma before it. It contrasts two ideas in a compound sentence.
>
> • Most volcanoes form near plate boundaries, **but** a few do not.

1 Fill in the blanks in the following sentences with *but* or *however*. Then find the sentences in the text "Earthquakes" and check your answers.

1 During a small earthquake, the earth simply shakes a little, and people may not even notice. _____, a strong movement can cause the earth to shake and roll violently.

2 Earthquakes can happen anywhere, _____ certain places have more earthquakes because they sit on tectonic plates that move frequently.

3 Scientists are not able to predict when an earthquake will happen. _____, they can identify the areas where earthquakes are most likely to occur.

4 We cannot stop tectonic plates from moving, _____ with accurate information and good planning, we can help people live more safely on our planet.

2 Use the ideas below and write your own sentences with *but* and *however*. Write your sentences on a separate piece of paper, following the example. Use correct punctuation and capital letters where necessary.

1 Volcanoes are destructive.

Volcanoes are destructive, but they also create new land on Earth.
Volcanoes are destructive. However, they also create new land on Earth.

2 California has earthquakes every day.

3 Many people think Los Angeles could fall into the ocean.

4 You may not feel Earth moving.

Task 5 USING CORRECT PARAGRAPH STRUCTURE

Academic paragraphs often have a specific structure:

- The first sentence of the paragraph is the **topic sentence**. It explains the main idea of the whole paragraph.
- The middle sentences of a paragraph are **supporting sentences**. They give details and examples that explain the main idea.
- The final sentence, or **concluding sentence**, ends the paragraph by reminding the reader about the main idea of the paragraph.

Not all academic paragraphs follow this structure, but many do. Becoming familiar with this pattern will help you read and understand academic texts more easily.

1 Reread paragraph 3 of the text "Earthquakes." Underline and label the topic sentence (*TS*). Next, bracket ([ ]) and label the supporting sentences (*SS*). Then draw two lines under the concluding sentence and label it (*CS*).

2 Read the following paragraph.

> There is no way to stop an earthquake, but there are several things you can do to prepare and protect yourself. Before an earthquake happens, you should make an emergency plan. You should also prepare an emergency supply kit with a battery-powered radio, a flashlight, and enough food and water for three days. During an earthquake, you should stay away from windows and tall furniture, get on the floor, cover your head, and hold on to something until the shaking stops. If you are outdoors, find a place away from buildings and trees, and get on the ground. After the earthquake stops, check to see if you have been hurt, and listen to the radio for instructions. If you are in an unsafe building, go outside. An earthquake can be a frightening experience, but knowing what to do before, during, and after it will help you stay safe.

3 Work with a partner. Answer the following questions about the paragraph in step 2:

   1 Does the paragraph have a topic sentence? If so, underline it, and label it (*TS*).

   2 How many supporting sentences are there? Bracket ([ ]) and label them (*SS*).

   3 Does the paragraph have a concluding sentence? If so, draw two lines under it, and label it (*CS*).

Chapter 2 Writing Assignment

Think about your favorite place on Earth. It can be, for example, a continent, an island, a mountain range, a river, a lake, or some other place. You may have traveled to this place, or perhaps you learned about it by reading a book, seeing a movie, or looking on the Internet. Follow the steps and guidelines below.

1 Have a short conversation with a partner. Tell each other about your favorite places.

2 Now write a paragraph about your favorite place.

1 Use the following topic sentence. Choose the word in parentheses that is the most appropriate for your place.

topic sentence: The most (interesting / exciting / beautiful) place on Earth that I know is _____.

2 Write four or five supporting sentences that show why your topic sentence is true.

3 Complete the following sentence, and add it to the end of your paragraph.

concluding sentence: For all these reasons, _____ is my favorite place.

Guidelines

- Use correct paragraph form and structure (see "Using Correct Paragraph Form," page 37, and "Using Correct Paragraph Structure," page 45).
- Include some new vocabulary you learned in this chapter.
- Vary your sentence structure. Use both simple and compound sentences (see "Writing Simple and Compound Sentences," page 31).
- Try to include some prepositional phrases (see the Language Focus task, page 30).
- Use pronoun reference correctly (see the Language Focus task, page 43).
- Include at least one sentence using *but* or *however* to show contrast (see the Language Focus task, page 44).

---

3 When you finish writing, exchange paragraphs with a partner and read each other's work. Then discuss the following questions about both paragraphs:

1 Are your favorite places similar or very different?
2 Does your partner's paragraph have correct form?
3 Do the supporting sentences explain the topic sentence? Are there any sentences that do not?

4 Make any changes to your paragraph that you think will improve it.

Unit 2

Water on Earth

In this unit, we look at the importance of water to life on Earth. In Chapter 3, we examine the natural process that continues to recycle water on our planet. We also focus on the sources of freshwater, such as rivers, lakes, and glaciers. In Chapter 4, we discuss Earth's oceans and the activity of currents and waves.

Previewing the unit

Read the contents page for Unit 2, and do the following activities.

Chapter 3: Earth's Water Supply

This chapter describes the water cycle and the sources of water on Earth. It focuses on our planet's freshwater supply.

Look at these photographs and discuss the questions below in a small group.

a _____   b _____   c _____

1 Each photograph shows a different type of water feature on Earth. Do you know the general names of any of these types? If so, write the names under the appropriate photos. Then check your answers at the bottom of the page.

2 How are these water features similar to each other? How are they different?

3 Are there any important water features where you live? If so, what are they?

4 Have you ever visited a famous water feature? If so, talk about your experience.

Chapter 4: Earth's Oceans

This chapter examines the oceans on our planet and the role they play in our lives.

1 | Discuss the following questions in small groups:

   1 Did you ever swim in an ocean? If so, how was it different from swimming in other places?

   2 Did you ever try an ocean sport such as sailing, surfing, or scuba diving? If so, describe how the ocean looked at that time. What sounds did you hear?

2 | The words in the left column below all have a connection with oceans. Match each word on the left with its definition on the right. Then check your answers at the bottom of the page.

_____ 1 the Pacific   **a** winds that blow from west to east and affect the ocean

_____ 2 salty   **b** a famous explorer who named the Pacific Ocean

_____ 3 tsunami   **c** a description of the taste of ocean water

_____ 4 Magellan   **d** Earth's largest ocean

_____ 5 the westerlies   **e** a very big and dangerous ocean wave

Answers to Chapter 4, step 2: **1** d, **2** c, **3** e, **4** b, **5** a

Answers to Chapter 3, step 1, 1: **a** lake, **b** river, **c** glacier.

Unit Contents 2

Preparing to read

1 | You are going to read a text about Earth's water cycle. First, look at the diagram of the water cycle on page 52. Then think back to what you learned in Chapter 1 about the rock cycle. What do you think the word *cycle* means?

2 | Read the following information from the text "The Water Cycle." Then answer the questions below with a partner.

> We call our planet Earth, but many people say that we should call it Water because water covers more than 70 percent of our planet. Water is essential to life on Earth. We drink it, swim in it, clean with it, and use it in many other ways. Surprisingly, the amount of water on Earth does not decrease even though we use so much of it every day.

1 Why would *Water* be a good name for our planet?

2 Name some places where you can find water on our planet.

3 What do you think the word *essential* means? Use the context to help you guess.

4 Make a list of all the ways you used water yesterday.

5 Compare your list with your partner's. Who do you think used more water? Were you surprised at how much water you used in one day?

6 What do you think the word *decrease* means? Use the context to help you guess.

7 We use a lot of water every day, but the total amount of water on Earth does not change. Why do you think our planet never runs out of water?

Now read

Now read the text "The Water Cycle." When you finish, turn to the tasks on page 53.

Earth's Water Supply

1 THE WATER CYCLE

We call our planet Earth, but many people say that we should call it Water because water covers more than 70 percent of our planet. Water is essential to life on Earth. We drink it, swim in it, clean with it, and use it in many other ways. Surprisingly, the amount of water on Earth does not decrease even though we use so much of it every day. This is because nature recycles water in a process called the water cycle (also called the hydrologic cycle). The water cycle is the movement of water from Earth into the atmosphere and back to Earth again.

1

What are the steps of the water cycle?

Energy from the sun produces **evaporation**, the first step in the water cycle. This is the process that changes water from a liquid to a gas. When the sun heats water, some of it turns into a gas called water vapor. Water evaporates anywhere there is sun and water. Most evaporation of water on Earth is from the oceans, but there is also evaporation from lakes, rivers, and even wet skin and clothing.

2

evaporation
the process that changes a heated liquid to a gas

In the second step, water vapor rises into the atmosphere, where it 3
cools and changes back into droplets (very small drops) of liquid water.
This process is called **condensation**. When water vapor condenses, it
forms clouds.

In the third step of the water cycle, the water droplets combine 4
(join together) to form larger drops that fall to earth as precipitation
(rain, snow, or hail). Some of this water goes into the ground, and some
of it goes into lakes, rivers, and oceans. Eventually, the water that has
come back to Earth will evaporate and rise into the atmosphere, and
the water cycle will continue.

How long is the water cycle?

The shortest water cycle on Earth occurs in tropical rain forests, which 5
are near the equator. In this wet environment, the whole water cycle
happens in just one day. In contrast, the slowest water cycle occurs in
deserts, which are very dry. It may not rain for years in a desert location, so it can take years to go through the whole cycle.

Water on Earth is always moving. It flows down rivers, travels across 6
the oceans, evaporates into the atmosphere, and falls to Earth as rain
and snow. The total amount of water on Earth stays the same year after
year because of the water cycle. In fact, the water on Earth now is the
same water that was on our planet millions of years ago. That means
the glass of water you drank today was actually millions of years old.

Figure 3.1
The water cycle

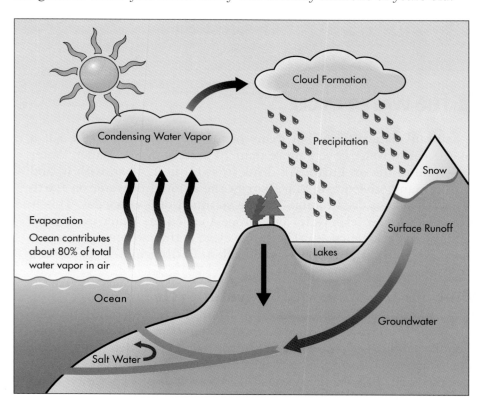

After you read

Task 1 TEST TAKING: UNDERSTANDING TEST QUESTIONS

You will often need to answer test questions about a text you have read. In order to answer correctly, think carefully about each question. First, identify the key words, or important words, in the question. Then decide what the question is asking. Here are some guidelines to help you:

- An answer to a *where?* question should include a place name or a description of a place.

  Q: Where is the Amazon River?
  A: It's in South America.

  Q: Where does the slowest water cycle occur?
  A: It occurs in deserts, which are very dry.

- An answer to a *why?* question should include an explanation or a reason for something.

  Q: Why does the amount of water on Earth always stay the same?
  A: The amount of water stays the same because nature recycles it.

- An answer to questions with *how many?* or *how much?* usually includes a number.

  Q: How much of our planet is covered by land?
  A: Less than 30 percent of our planet is covered by land.

1 Read the questions below. First, underline the key words and decide what each question is asking. Then write the answers on a separate piece of paper, using information from the text "The Water Cycle."

    1 How much of Earth is covered by water?

    2 How many steps does the water cycle have?

    3 Where does water evaporate from?

    4 Why does water vapor change back to liquid water?

    5 Where is the fastest water cycle on Earth?

    6 Why is the water on Earth today actually millions of years old?

2 Now write two more questions about the text.

3 Exchange your questions with a partner and answer each other's questions.

Task 2 SEQUENCING

Scientific information often includes a process, or a series of steps. To understand a process, you need to understand each of the steps and the correct sequence (order) of the steps.

1 Reread paragraphs 2–4 of the text "The Water Cycle," and review Figure 3.1. Then work with a partner. Number the following steps of the water cycle in the correct order (1–8). Try not to look back at the text.

_____ The water vapor moves up into the atmosphere.

_____ Some of the raindrops fall into lakes, rivers, and oceans.

_____ The sun comes out and begins to warm the water in the ocean again.

_____ The water vapor cools and changes into droplets of water.

_____ The small water droplets inside the cloud combine into bigger water drops, which fall from the cloud as rain.

_____ Some of the water in the ocean becomes water vapor.

_1_ The sun heats the water in an ocean.

_____ A cloud forms.

2 Complete the diagram of the water cycle below. Draw the sequence in step 1 and label the steps. Include arrows to show the process.

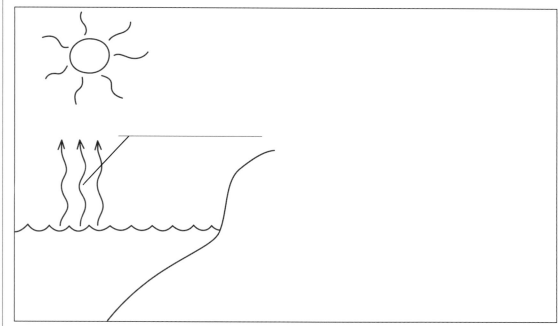

The water cycle

3 Look back at Figure 3.1 on page 52 to check your work.

Task 3 BUILDING VOCABULARY: ANTONYMS

> **Antonyms** are words that have opposite meanings. For example, *cold* and *hot* are antonyms. Learning antonyms is a good way to add words to your vocabulary.

1 | All of the words below are from the text "The Water Cycle." Match each word in the left column below with its antonym on the right.

_____	**1** cools	**a**	slowest
_____	**2** rise	**b**	large
_____	**3** evaporation	**c**	dry
_____	**4** fastest	**d**	heats
_____	**5** wet	**e**	fall
_____	**6** small	**f**	condensation

2 | Choose three pairs of antonyms from step 1. On a separate piece of paper, use the antonyms to write sentences with *but* and *however*. Follow this example:

In Quito, Ecuador, the wettest month is April, but the driest month is July.

In Quito, Ecuador, the wettest month is April. However, the driest month is July.

Task 4 BUILDING VOCABULARY: SUFFIXES THAT CHANGE VERBS INTO NOUNS

> You can change many verbs into nouns by adding a **suffix**, or ending. Two common suffixes that change verbs into nouns are *-ment* and *-ion / -ation*. If the verb ends in *-e*, drop the *-e* before adding the suffix.
>
> Look at these examples:
>
> | **Verb** | **Noun** |
> |---|---|
> | erupt | erup**tion** |
> | contribute | contribu**tion** |
> | inform | informa**tion** |
> | argue | argu**ment** |
> | assign | assign**ment** |

1 Find and circle the noun forms of the following verbs in the text "The Water Cycle." Then write each noun next to the appropriate verb below.

Verb	**Noun Form**
1 move	_____ (par. 1)
2 evaporate	_____ (par. 2)
3 condense	_____ (par. 3)
4 locate	_____ (par. 5)

2 Decide if each sentence below is missing a noun or a verb and write *n.* or *v.* in the blank. Then circle the correct word to complete each sentence.

_____ **1** Our teachers always (assign / assignment) a lot of homework.

_____ **2** Last year I saw a volcanic (erupt / eruption). It was amazing!

_____ **3** In an emergency, listen to the radio for (inform / information).

_____ **4** If you leave a glass of water in the sun, it will (evaporate / evaporation). Then the glass will be empty.

_____ **5** The students found the (locate / location) of the Sahara Desert on a map.

_____ **6** The water in a river (movement / moves) downhill until it reaches the ocean.

Task 5   IDENTIFYING TOPIC SENTENCES

> Many paragraphs in academic English begin with a **topic sentence** that explains the main idea of the paragraph.

1 Look back at paragraphs 2, 3, and 4 of the text "The Water Cycle." Underline the topic sentence of each paragraph. Notice that by reading only these three topic sentences, you can understand the steps in the water cycle.

2   **1** Read the paragraph at the top of the next page.

   2 What is the main idea of the paragraph? Write it here: _____

   _____

   3 The paragraph is missing a topic sentence. Choose the correct topic sentence from the list below the paragraph.

_____. In fact, over half of Earth's plant species live in these very wet environments. We use many of the plants for food or medicine. There are more than 3,000 types of fruit in rain forests, including avocados, coconuts, and guavas. Tropical rain forests also contain a large number of vegetables, such as corn, potatoes, and yams, and spices like black pepper, chocolate, and cinnamon. In addition, 70 percent of the plants that can help fight cancer and other diseases are found in the rain forest. This rich plant life makes tropical rain forests a very important feature of Earth.

Check (✔) the best topic sentence for the paragraph above.

_____ **a** Tropical rain forests are an important part of the water cycle.

_____ **b** Many plants and animals live in tropical rainforests.

_____ **c** Tropical rain forests are home to a wide variety of plants.

3 Read the following paragraph. It is missing a topic sentence. Write one.

_____. The first type of desert is the hot desert. Most hot deserts are near the Tropic of Cancer or the Tropic of Capricorn. These deserts have high temperatures in the daytime, cooler temperatures at night, and just a little rain. Only a few plants can live in hot deserts. The second type of desert is the cold desert. Some of these deserts are near the Arctic, the most northern part of the world. Antarctica, the most southern part of the world, is also a cold desert. Some cold deserts have high temperatures in the summer but very cold temperatures in the winter. Others stay very cold all the time. Cold deserts have almost no rain but some snow. There are even fewer plants in cold deserts than in hot deserts. These differences clearly show that although all deserts are dry, they are not all the same.

4 Compare your topic sentences with a partner's.

Preparing to read

THINKING ABOUT THE TOPIC BEFORE YOU READ

Discuss the following questions with a partner or in a small group:

1 Freshwater is water that does not have salt in it. Do you think Earth has more freshwater or salt water?

2 Do you think more of our planet's freshwater is under the ground or on the surface?

3 Where do you get your drinking water?

EXAMINING GRAPHIC MATERIAL

Before reading a text, it is helpful to look at any graphs, charts, or diagrams. This will give you an idea of the content (the information that the text contains).

The text you are going to read is about the distribution of freshwater and salt water on our planet. Look at Figure 3.2 on page 59 and answer the following questions with a partner.

1 Is most of the water on our planet freshwater or salt water?

2 How much of Earth's water is in the oceans?

3 How much of the freshwater is under the ground (groundwater)?

4 How much of it is in the form of ice?

5 How much freshwater is accessible, or easy to get and use?

Now read

Now read the text "Groundwater and Surface Water." When you finish, turn to the tasks on page 61.

2 GROUNDWATER AND SURFACE WATER

Fresh, clean water is essential to life on Earth. Plants, animals, and humans all need it to survive. People grow plants for food, and that requires a lot of water. In fact, as much as four-fifths of the world's freshwater supply is used for agriculture. To stay healthy, people also have to drink a lot of freshwater every day.

Unfortunately, most of the water on our planet (almost 97 percent) is not freshwater but salt water. Only about 3 percent is freshwater, and more than three-quarters of that water is frozen, or ice. This means that only a small amount of the water on Earth is freshwater that we can drink. Most of this drinkable water is under the ground (groundwater); only about 1 percent is on the surface (surface water) and accessible.

Groundwater

Deep inside the lithosphere are billions of liters of freshwater. When rain or snow falls from the sky, some of it goes down into the ground and fills the spaces between the sand and rocks. As the water moves deeper into the ground, it reaches an area where all the spaces are full of water. This area is called the zone of saturation. Sometimes there is enough groundwater for people to dig a well and pump the water out so they can use it. Such large areas of groundwater are called **aquifers**. Sometimes the water in an aquifer leaks out of cracks in the earth and up to the surface, where it goes into lakes and rivers.

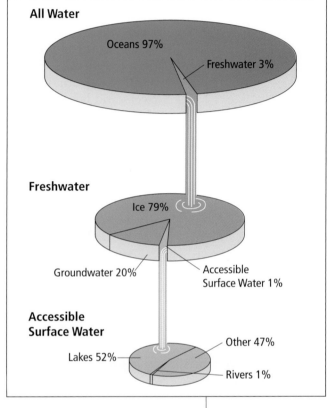

Figure 3.2 The distribution of water on Earth

aquifer

an area of rock and soil that holds a lot of water that can be pumped out and used

Surface water in lakes

Lakes are an important source of accessible freshwater. There are millions of lakes on Earth, and almost half of them are in Canada. However, the largest lake on Earth is Lake Baikal in Siberia. It contains 20 percent of all the freshwater on the surface of our planet. The water in a lake is fairly calm and quiet because it is surrounded by land on all sides. Most lakes are in areas that glaciers covered in the past. Some lakes form when rocks stop a river from flowing. Lakes also form when rainwater fills the opening of an extinct volcano.

Surface water in rivers

Rivers are another source of freshwater. When rain or snow falls in the mountains, some of the water goes into the ground and some of it stays on the surface and flows downhill. This movement often creates a small mountain stream, which may eventually join with other streams to form a river. A young river flows quickly downhill and changes the shape of the land. It cuts a path down the mountain and forms a V-shaped valley. As the valley grows larger and the mountain becomes less steep, the river becomes deeper and wider. Finally, the river reaches flatter land, where it flows more slowly until it reaches the ocean. The largest river in the world is the Amazon River. In fact, the Amazon contains more than one-fifth of the world's total river water.

If the groundwater under the lithosphere and the surface water in rivers and lakes disappeared, most of the life on our planet would probably disappear, too. Thanks to the water cycle, Earth has a constant supply of freshwater. It is extremely important to protect this valuable resource from pollution. It is also important to conserve water, that is, to avoid using too much. If we are careful, future generations will also have access to fresh, clean water for everyday use.

Bottled Water or Tap Water?

Where does the water you drink come from? Do you drink tap water from the faucet, or do you drink bottled water? Many people think that bottled water is cleaner and safer than tap water. Surprisingly, this is usually not true. In some parts of the world, where the public water supply may be polluted, bottled water is a good choice. In most parts of the world, however, the water supply is clean, safe, and easily accessible.

Bottled water is very popular in several countries. For example, more than 50 percent of Americans, Canadians, and Italians drink it. Some people drink bottled water because they think it is more natural. The labels on the bottles often show mountain streams and beautiful waterfalls, so people think this water comes directly from nature. In fact, more than 25 percent of all bottled water sold in the United States is purified water that comes from a faucet, not a mountain stream. Other people drink bottled water because they think it tastes better than tap water. However, in blind taste tests, most people cannot taste the difference. Therefore, if you do have access to a good water supply, you may want to turn on the faucet for your next drink. You'll save money, and the water will be clean, safe, and good-tasting.

After you read

Task 1 TEST TAKING: ANSWERING MULTIPLE CHOICE QUESTIONS

When you answer multiple choice questions, pay special attention to the questions that include the word *not*.

Example: Which one of the following is not a step in the water cycle?
   a evaporation
   b saturation
   c condensation

In the example, choices *a* and *c* (*evaporation* and *condensation*) are steps in the water cycle. The correct answer is *b*, because *saturation* is not a step.

Review "Test Taking: Answering Multiple Choice Questions" on page 21. Then answer the questions below, based on information in the text "Groundwater and Surface Water." Pay special attention to the questions with *not*. Compare your answers with a partner.

1 How much of the freshwater on Earth is accessible surface water that we can drink?
   a about 97 percent
   b about 75 percent
   c about 3 percent
   d about 1 percent

2 Most of the freshwater on our planet is _____.
   a under the ground
   b frozen
   c in oceans
   d in lakes

3 An aquifer is _____.
   a under the ground
   b on the surface
   c very small
   d sand and rocks

4 Which one of the following is not an example of surface water?
   a a river
   b a lake
   c an aquifer
   d an ocean

5 Which phrase does not describe lakes?
   a freshwater
   b surrounded by land
   c calm water
   d flow from mountains to the ocean

6 Rivers do not _____.
   a flow downhill
   b change the shape of the land
   c create U-shaped valleys
   d flow into oceans

Task 2 NOTE TAKING: MAPPING

Some people take notes on a text by making a map of the content. One way to do this is to draw lines and circles to show relationships among the facts and ideas.

1 The illustration below is the beginning of a map of the text "Groundwater and Surface Water." The circle in the center is large and its content is general. Away from the center, the circles become smaller and their content becomes more specific.

2 Complete the map. Fill in the blank circles with information from the text. Then compare your map with a partner's.

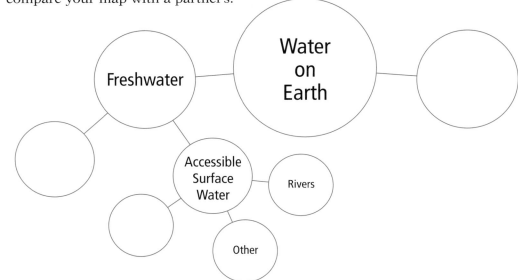

Task 3 CONDUCTING A SURVEY

Surveys are often used in academic research to get information about people's opinions and behaviors.

Conduct a survey to answer this question: Can most people tell the difference between bottled water and tap water in a blind taste test? Ask at least six people to participate.

1 Prepare four cups of water for each person in your survey. Fill three cups with bottled water and one cup with tap water. Label the cups A, B, C, and D.

2 Have each person drink from the four cups and tell you which cup they think contains tap water. Record their names and answers on a separate piece of paper.

3 How many people identified the tap water correctly? Make a pie chart to show the results of your survey. Share the results with the class.

Task 4 LANGUAGE FOCUS: COUNTABLE AND UNCOUNTABLE NOUNS

English nouns can be divided into two groups:

Countable nouns are things that we can count.

• Countable nouns have both singular and plural forms (*river / rivers*).

• Countable nouns can take a determiner: *a, an, the,* or a number.
  A river is a source of freshwater.
  The longest **river** in Canada is the Mackenzie River.
  Two rivers in Russia are the **Volga River** and the **Don River**.

Uncountable nouns are things that cannot be counted.

• Uncountable nouns are often:

Liquids	Gases	Ideas	Things made up of little pieces
water	oxygen	love	rice
coffee	carbon dioxide	peace	dust

• Uncountable nouns do not have plural forms. They take singular verbs.
  Water is essential for life on Earth.
  When **water condenses**, it forms clouds.

• Uncountable nouns do not take *a, an,* or a number. You can use the noun alone or with *the*.
  CORRECT: **Water** is dripping from the faucet.
            The water in a lake is freshwater.
  INCORRECT: A water is good for your health.

1 Reread paragraph 3 of the text "Groundwater and Surface Water." Find and circle three countable nouns and three uncountable nouns. Write the words in the blanks.

Countable nouns: _____ _____ _____

Uncountable nouns: _____ _____ _____

2 Read the following sentences. Label each underlined noun either *C* (countable) or *U* (uncountable).

1 The United States is between two <u>oceans</u>: the Atlantic Ocean and the Pacific Ocean.

2 When Mount Vesuvius erupted, <u>lava</u> covered the city of Pompeii, Italy.

3 Most of Antarctica has a thick cover of <u>ice</u>.

4 The Nile <u>River</u> and the Amazon River are two of the longest rivers on Earth.

5 An example of an <u>aquifer</u> is the Ogallala Aquifer in the midwestern part of the United States.

Task 5 WORKING WITH STATISTICS

Statistics are numerical facts, or facts that are stated as numbers. Writers of academic texts often use statistics to support their ideas. Statistics can be stated in whole numbers (*50, 1,000, 32 billion*), fractions (*one-third, one-half, four-fifths*), or percentages (*33%, 50%, 80%*). Understanding the statistics in a text will help you understand the ideas.

1 Answer the questions below. Base your answers on the statistics in the text "Groundwater and Surface Water" and the boxed text "Bottled Water or Tap Water?"

   1 Do people use more water for agriculture or for drinking? _____

   2 What percentage of water on Earth is freshwater? _____

   3 Is most freshwater in liquid form or frozen? _____

   4 Does all bottled water come from natural sources, such as streams? _____

2 Sometimes you will have to answer a question about a statistic in a text with a different form of the number. For example:

   Text: **Fifty percent** of people in Canada drink bottled water.
   Question: **What fraction** of people in Canada drink bottled water?
   Answer: one-half (1/2)

Match the fractions in the right column below with their corresponding percentages in the left column.

   _____ 80 percent   **a** one-fourth (1/4)

   _____ 50 percent   **b** one-tenth (1/10)

   _____ 33 percent   **c** four-fifths (4/5)

   _____ 20 percent   **d** one-fifth (1/5)

   _____ 25 percent   **e** one-third (1/3)

   _____ 10 percent   **f** one-half (1/2)

3 Answer the questions below. Base your answers on the statistics in the text "Groundwater and Surface Water" and the boxed text "Bottled Water or Tap Water?"

   1 What percentage of the world's freshwater supply is used for agriculture? _____

   2 What fraction of Earth's surface freshwater is found in Lake Baikal? _____

   3 What percentage of the world's lakes is in Canada? _____

   4 What fraction of bottled water in the United States is purified water? _____

4 Compare your answers to steps 1–3 with a partner's.

Task 6 IDENTIFYING SUPPORTING SENTENCES

Remember that **supporting sentences** follow the topic sentence. They support the topic sentence by explaining the main idea in more detail.

1 Read the following sentences. Divide the sentences into two groups (Set A and Set B), according to the main idea. Write the sentences in the chart below. Then write the main idea for each set.

1 If any faucet is leaking, have it fixed.
2 Many people believe that the Nile River is the longest river in the world.
3 Try to take shorter showers.
4 It is more than 6,500 kilometers long and flows through nine countries.
5 Wait until you have a full load of laundry before you run your washing machine.
6 The Yangtze River is the most famous river in China.
7 Remember to check your home for leaky faucets.
8 It is about 4,990 kilometers long and divides north China and south China.

Set A
Main idea: _____

• *Remember to check your home for leaky faucets.*

• _____

• _____

• _____

Set B
Main idea: _____

• _____

• _____

• _____

• _____

2 Use the sentences in either Set A or Set B to write a paragraph. First, write a topic sentence that states the main idea. Then put the supporting sentences in a logical order. (Several orders are possible.)

3 Compare your paragraph with a partner's.

Preparing to read

INCREASING YOUR READING SPEED

Academic classes often require a lot of reading. However, there is not always time to read every text slowly and carefully. Reading speed can be as important as reading comprehension. Here are some strategies for increasing your reading speed:

- Read the text straight through. Do not go back to any parts of it.
- Do not stop to look up words in a dictionary.
- Skip over words you do not know if they do not seem important.
- Try to guess the meaning of words that seem important.
- Slow down a little to understand important parts, such as definitions and main ideas.

1 | Read the text "Glaciers" using the strategies in the box. For this task, do not read the boxed text, "Facts About Glaciers," on page 68.

Before you begin, fill in your starting time.   Starting time: _____

2 | Fill in the time you finished.   Finishing time: _____

Then calculate your reading speed:
   Number of words in the text (418) ÷
   Number of minutes it took you to   Reading speed: _____
   read the text = your reading speed

Your reading speed = the number of words you can read per minute.

3 | Check your reading comprehension. Circle the correct answers without looking at the text.

   1 Glaciers are made of:
      a fresh and salt water   **b** soil and rocks   **c** layers of ice

   2 Glaciers can move:
      a rocks and soil   **b** people and animals   **c** rivers and oceans

   3 Glaciers move:
      a quickly   **b** slowly   **c** not at all

Now read

Now read the text "Glaciers" again, including the boxed text. Then check your answers to step 3 above. When you finish, turn to the tasks on page 69.

3 GLACIERS

In a small town in Alberta, Canada, there is a giant rock called Big Rock. This rock is 9 meters high, 41 meters long, and 18 meters wide. It weighs almost 14,970 metric tons. Thousands of years ago, Big Rock moved approximately 400 kilometers to its present location. How could such a huge rock move so far? It actually got a ride from a glacier. 1

Glaciers are layers of ice that move. Some people call them rivers of ice. Glaciers form when snow falls and does not melt. More snow falls and presses down until the snow underneath becomes ice. This cycle continues until the thick layers of ice become so heavy that they begin to slide over the ground. When they begin moving, the layers of ice are called a glacier. They slide slowly down hills and valleys until they melt or reach the ocean. 2

Glaciers may move slowly, but they are powerful. Over time they can carve, or cut out, deep valleys and create beautiful landscapes. They are strong enough to move large amounts of soil and pull rocks of all sizes out of the ground. This is called *plucking*. Several glaciers can surround a mountain and pluck rocks from all sides. This is the process that created the sharp mountaintop of the Matterhorn in Switzerland. 3

A glacier in the Alps, Switzerland

Since glaciers are usually wider than rivers, they create wide U-shaped valleys, not narrow V-shaped ones, as they move across the land. Sometimes a glacier 4 will carve a U-shaped valley near the ocean. After the glacier melts, the ocean water sometimes fills these valleys. This creates a landform called a **fjord** ('fee-YORD'). Norway has the world's most famous and beautiful fjords, but there are also fjords in Alaska and Japan.

fjord
a valley near the ocean, originally created by a glacier, that has filled with ocean water

Kayakers at Kenai Fjords National Park, Alaska, U.S.

climate

the usual weather
conditions in a
particular place

Scientists study glaciers to learn about world **climates** and climate   5
change. They measure how fast glaciers move and changes in their size.
Today, scientists report that Earth's glaciers are melting more quickly
than they have in the past 100 years. This is an important sign that
Earth has been warming up.

Glaciers are also important because they contain more than 75 per-   6
cent of all the freshwater on our planet. When they melt, they provide
drinking water and water for crops in some dry parts of the world.
However, some glaciers are melting too quickly. They are decreasing in
size, and eventually they will disappear. As a result, many people will
lose their main source of water. Scientists and environmentalists all
over the world are trying to solve this serious problem.

Facts About Glaciers

- Today, glaciers cover about 10 percent of the land on Earth.

- Twenty thousand years ago, glaciers covered 32 percent of the
  land on Earth.

- If all the glaciers on Earth melted today, the height of the
  oceans would increase by about 70 meters.

- Some glaciers in the Arctic contain ice that is more than
  100,000 years old.

- The Lambert Glacier in Antarctica is the largest glacier in the
  world. It is about 80 kilometers wide and 500 kilometers long.

- The Kutiah Glacier in Pakistan is one of the fastest-moving
  glaciers. In 1953, it moved more than 12 kilometers in three
  months (an average of about 112 meters per day).

Sources: U.S. Geological Survey
         National Snow and Ice Data Center

After you read

Task 1 READING FOR MAIN IDEAS

1| Look back at the text "Glaciers." Write the number of the paragraph that discusses each of the following main ideas.

1 Glaciers create U-shaped valleys, and some of these eventually become fjords. par. _____

2 Glaciers are large, slow-moving layers of ice. par. _____

3 Studying glaciers can provide information about world climates. par. _____

4 Glaciers can move huge rocks hundreds of kilometers. par. _____

5 Glaciers can create valleys, pull rocks out of the ground, and shape mountains. par. _____

2| Check (✔) the sentence that expresses the main idea of the whole text.

_____ 1 Glaciers are very powerful, and they can lift heavy objects.

_____ 2 Glaciers are melting quickly, and we need to find a way to save them.

_____ 3 Glaciers are layers of ice that shape the land, and they can teach us about climate.

_____ 4 Glaciers are layers of ice that move slowly over the land.

Task 2 SCANNING FOR DETAILS

Scanning is helpful when you study for a test or prepare a writing assignment. Scanning a text means reading quickly to find specific information. When you scan, you do not read every word. Your eyes pass over the text, stopping only when you find the information you need.

Sometimes scanning for certain signals in a text will help you find information. For example, to find a place name, scan for capital letters. To find an amount or a measurement, scan for numbers or percent symbols (%).

Scan the text "Glaciers" and the boxed text "Facts About Glaciers" to find the following information.

1 Where is Big Rock located? _____

2 How long is Big Rock? _____

3 How many kilometers did Big Rock move? _____

4 What is the shape of a valley that a glacier creates? _____

5 What are three places that have fjords? _____ _____ _____

6 How much of Earth do glaciers cover today? _____

7 What is the name of the largest glacier on Earth? _____

8 Where is the Kutiah Glacier? _____

Task 3 LANGUAGE FOCUS: SUBJECT-VERB AGREEMENT

- Singular subjects take singular verbs. Remember that in the present tense, third-person singular verbs end in -s or -es.

  subject verb   subject verb
  Big Rock weighs almost 14,970 metric tons. **It is** 9 meters high.

  subject verb
  A glacier carves deep valleys as it slides over the ground.

- Plural subjects take plural verbs. Plural verbs do not end in -s.

  subject verb
  Scientists study glaciers to learn about world climates.

- Uncountable nouns take singular verbs.

  subject verb
  Water covers 97 percent of Earth's surface.

Complete the following sentences with the correct form of the verb in parentheses.

1 A glacier _____ (form) when the snow in an area does not melt. Over time, this snow _____ (turn) into ice.
2 In some glaciers, the ice _____ (be) thousands of years old.
3 Glaciers _____ (contain) more than 75 percent of Earth's freshwater.
4 Every continent _____ (have) glaciers except Australia.

Task 4 EXAMINING SUPPORTING SENTENCES AND EXAMPLES

There are different ways to support the topic sentence in a paragraph. One way is to state a few important ideas and then explain each one more fully with examples.

Read the paragraph below and do the following: Underline the topic sentence; highlight the two supporting sentences; highlight the examples in a different color. Compare your work with a partner's.

Glaciers change the surface of our planet in different ways. One way is by shaping the land. For example, glaciers carve U-shaped valleys and form sharp mountaintops. Glaciers can also move big rocks to other locations. Another way glaciers change Earth is by creating lakes. For instance, Mirror Lake and the Great Lakes in the United States were formed by glaciers. Lake Louise in Canada is another example. Earth would look very different without the work of glaciers.

Chapter 3   Writing Assignment

In this assignment, you will write a paragraph that explains the following sentence:

Rivers and lakes affect our lives in many ways.

Use information from this chapter and your own ideas. Follow the steps and guidelines below.

1 Work in a small group. Make a list of the different ways (both good and bad) that rivers and lakes affect people's lives. Try to list at least eight ways.

2 Then, on your own, write a topic sentence that states the main idea for the paragraph.

3 Choose two or three ideas from your group's list that will support your topic sentence. Think of at least one example for each idea. Take notes to help you remember your examples.

4 Now write the paragraph.

  1 Following your topic sentence, write four to six supporting sentences based on the ideas and examples you chose in step 3. You can use phrases such as *one way* and *another way* to introduce the ideas. To introduce the examples, you can use *for example* and *for instance*. Review the paragraph in "Examining Supporting Sentences and Examples" on page 70 to see how these phrases are used.

  2 End your paragraph with the following concluding sentence:

    These are just a few of the ways that rivers and lakes influence our lives.

Guidelines
- Use correct paragraph form and structure (see "Using Correct Paragraph Form," page 37, and "Using Correct Paragraph Structure," page 45).
- Try to include some new vocabulary you learned in this chapter.
- Be sure the subject and verb in each sentence agree with each other (see the Language Focus task, page 70).

---

5 When you finish writing, exchange paragraphs with a partner and read each other's work. Then discuss the following questions about both paragraphs:

  1 Which idea in your partner's paragraph do you think is the most interesting?

  2 Does your partner's paragraph use correct form?

  3 Does the paragraph have a topic sentence that states the main idea?

  4 Do the supporting sentences support the topic sentence? Are there any sentences that do not?

  5 Make any changes to your paragraph that you think would improve it.

Preparing to read

THINKING ABOUT THE TOPIC BEFORE YOU READ

You are going to read a text about the oceans on Earth. How much do you know about this topic? Discuss the following questions in a small group.

1 How many oceans are there? Name the ones you know.
2 In what ways are oceans different from rivers and lakes?
3 How does ocean water taste?
4 What are some living things you can find in the ocean?
5 Why are oceans an important part of life on our planet?

BUILDING BACKGROUND KNOWLEDGE ABOUT THE TOPIC

The word *coast* refers to land that is next to or close to an ocean. Read the following list of facts about coastal areas on Earth. Then discuss the questions below with your classmates.

Facts About Coastal Areas

- About 60 percent of the people on Earth live less than 100 kilometers from an ocean.
- Almost two-thirds of the world's largest cities are in coastal areas.
- Since 1970, almost 50 percent of the construction of new homes and businesses in the United States has been in areas along the coasts.
- By 2010, half the people in the United States will live in coastal areas.

---

1 Why do so many people live near an ocean?
2 What are some advantages of living near an ocean?
3 When many people live near an ocean, what is the effect on the ocean's water and animals?
4 If the water level of the oceans rises, how will people's lives be affected?

Now read

Now read the text "Oceans." When you finish, turn to the tasks on page 75.

Earth's Oceans

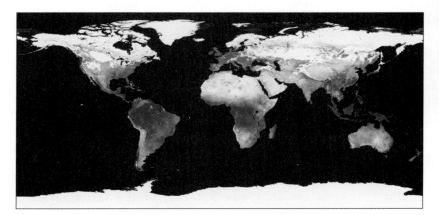

1 OCEANS

One nickname for Earth is the "blue planet" because from outer space, all the ocean water makes the planet look blue. There are four main oceans: the Pacific, the Atlantic, the Indian, and the Arctic. Many scientists include the Southern Ocean, also called the Antarctic Ocean, as a fifth ocean. Together, the oceans cover more than 70 percent of Earth's surface, and they flow into each other.* Therefore, from outer space it looks as if Earth has one huge blue ocean.

1

The main oceans

The Pacific is the largest and deepest of the main oceans. It contains approximately half the ocean water on our planet. When the explorer Ferdinand Magellan first sailed on this huge ocean, it was a calm day. That's why he named the ocean *Mar Pacífico*, which means "peaceful ocean" or "calm ocean" in Portuguese. Today, however, we know that the Pacific Ocean can be quite violent because of its frequent earthquakes and volcanic eruptions.

2

The Atlantic Ocean is the second-largest ocean. It covers about a fifth of Earth's surface. The Indian Ocean is the calmest ocean. It is a little smaller than the Atlantic. The Arctic Ocean is Earth's smallest ocean.

3

The salinity of oceans

If you swim in the ocean, you'll notice right away that the water is salty. Ocean water is about 96.5 percent water and 3.5 percent salt. The **salinity** of an ocean varies, depending on two main factors: the

4

salinity
a measure of the amount of salt in ocean water

---

* You can find the oceans discussed in this chapter on the map of the world on pages 210–211.

amount of evaporation and the amount of freshwater that is added. As ocean water evaporates, it leaves salt behind. Oceans that have a lot of evaporation are saltier than oceans that have less. When rivers or rain bring freshwater to an ocean, the ocean becomes less salty because the freshwater dilutes, or weakens, the salt.

In areas near the **equator**, where the heat of the sun causes a lot   5
of evaporation and there is not a lot of rain, there are high levels of salinity in the warm ocean water. In cold areas near the **North Pole** and the **South Pole**, there is less evaporation, and the ocean receives freshwater from melting glaciers. Therefore, salinity is lower in polar areas. The lowest salinity levels occur where large rivers empty into an ocean. That's why the place where the giant Amazon River flows into the Atlantic Ocean is less salty than the rest of the ocean.

The role of oceans in our lives

Although oceans do not provide our drinking water, they affect us in   6
many ways. First, oceans are an important part of the water cycle, because most of the evaporation on Earth is from ocean water. Oceans also provide us with food and jobs. Millions of people work in the fishing industry, shipbuilding, ocean science, the U.S. Navy, and the U.S. Coast Guard. In addition, the ocean is the home of a great many of our planet's plants and animals. Finally, coastal areas are popular places to live. Today, about 60 percent of the world's people live close to an ocean. Since oceans are clearly an essential part of life on Earth, we should pay careful attention to any changes or problems that occur in ocean water.

Ferdinand Magellan

the equator

an imaginary line around Earth that divides it into two equal halves: the Northern and Southern hemispheres

North Pole

Earth's northernmost point, which is located in the Arctic Ocean

South Pole

Earth's southernmost point, which is located in Antarctica

Ferdinand Magellan

Ferdinand Magellan (1480–1521) was a Portuguese explorer with a dream. He wanted to sail a ship all the way around the world, something no explorer had ever done. When Magellan and other European sailors of his time sailed to Asia, they always traveled south along the coast of Africa and then east, around Africa's Cape of Good Hope. Magellan had an idea: Maybe it was possible to reach Asia by sailing west instead.

On September 20, 1519, Magellan set sail from Spain with five ships. They sailed across the Atlantic Ocean, down the coast of South America, and through the narrow passage at the southern tip of the continent. On the other side was a huge ocean, which Magellan named *Mar Pacífico*. Although the Pacific was calm on that first day, the trip across it was terrible. Day after day, there was no land in sight. The men ran out of food and freshwater, and many became sick and died. The ships finally reached the island of Guam, and from there they sailed to the Philippines. Unfortunately, Magellan was killed there, and he never saw his dream come true. Only one of his ships was successful. It continued sailing west and reached Spain on September 6, 1522. It had traveled 50,610 miles and crossed three oceans.

After you read

Task 1 NOTE TAKING: LEARNING TO TAKE GOOD NOTES

Good notes can help you remember and review a text you have read.
People usually have their own ways of taking notes, but everyone should
follow these guidelines:

- Be sure to include all the important ideas and examples.
- Organize the notes in a logical way.
- Write only important words, not complete sentences.
- Use abbreviations and symbols.

Look at the notebook page below. It shows the beginning of a student's notes on the
text "Oceans." Based on the information you read, fill in the blanks to complete the
notes. Then compare your notes with a partner's.

Oceans

General info
    5 oceans: Pacific, _____, _____, Arctic, Southern
    Cover _____% of Earth's surface

Main oceans & features
    Pacific: largest, _____, often violent
    Atlantic: 2nd _____, covers _____ of Earth's surface
    Indian: calmest, _____ than Atlantic

Salinity (= saltiness)
    Ocean water = 96.5% water + _____ salt
    Depends on: 1) amount of _____
              2) amount of freshwater
    Higher near the equator, lower near the _____ & the
    places where _____

Importance of oceans
  Ex: 1. Role in water cycle
     2. Provide _____
     3. Provide jobs
     4. Home for many _____ + _____
     5. People like to live nearby

Task 2 USING A MAP KEY

Most maps have a key that helps you read them. The key explains the marks and symbols used on the map.

1 Study the map below. It shows general patterns of ocean salinity.* Read the key. What do the three colors show?

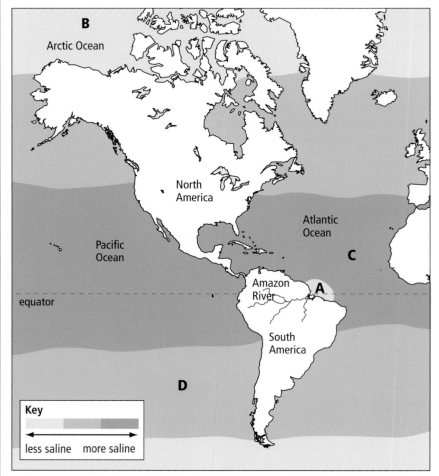

* Note that salinity levels vary within these general patterns.

2 Find the areas listed below on the map in step 1. Using the map and the key, decide on the level of salinity of each area. Write *L* (low), *M* (medium), or *H* (high).

1 _____ area A
2 _____ area B
3 _____ area C
4 _____ area D

3 Compare your answers with a partner's.

Task 3 LANGUAGE FOCUS: SUPERLATIVE ADJECTIVES

Use a **superlative adjective** to compare three or more people, places, or things in a group. Superlatives begin with *the*. Look at these examples:

- The Pacific is **the deepest** ocean in the world. It is deeper than all the other oceans.
- Some people think Columbus is **the most famous** explorer. They think he is more famous than Magellan or Vasco da Gama.

To form superlative adjectives, follow these guidelines:

> For **one-syllable adjectives**, add -*est*. If the adjective ends in *e*, add -*st*.
> deep ➜ the deepest
> wide ➜ the widest

> For **one-syllable adjectives that end with a single vowel and a consonant**, double the final consonant and add -*est*.
> hot ➜ the hottest
> big ➜ the biggest

> For **adjectives with two syllables or more**, add *the most* before the adjective.
> dangerous ➜ the most dangerous
> interesting ➜ the most interesting

> If an adjective ends in *y*, change the *y* to *i* and add -*est*.
> rocky ➜ the rockiest
> cloudy ➜ the cloudiest

> **Irregular adjectives** do not follow a pattern. Some common ones are:
> good ➜ the best
> bad ➜ the worst
> far ➜ the farthest

1 Reread the text "Oceans." Circle all the superlative adjectives. How many did you find?

2 Write the superlative form of each adjective below.
- **a** large _____
- **b** cold _____
- **c** small _____
- **d** salty _____
- **e** peaceful _____
- **f** important _____

3 Complete the sentences below with the correct forms of the superlative adjectives in the box. Use each adjective once.

calm	deep	small	successful	violent

1 The Pacific is _____*the deepest*_____ ocean on Earth. It is deeper than all the other oceans.

2 The Pacific is also _____ ocean. It has many earthquakes and volcanoes.

3 The Indian Ocean is _____ ocean. The water is usually quiet.

4 The Arctic Ocean is _____ ocean. All the other oceans are larger.

5 _____ ship in Magellan's group sailed all the way around the world.

Task 4   LANGUAGE FOCUS: *THEREFORE* AND *THAT'S WHY*

A sentence beginning with *therefore* or *that's why* explains the effect or result of something. The preceding sentence (the sentence that comes before) tells the cause of the result or effect. Look at these examples:

cause	effect (result)
Ocean water contains about 3.5 percent salt.	**Therefore, it tastes salty.**

cause	effect (result)
Ocean water contains about 3.5 percent salt.	**That's why it tastes salty.**

Notice that *therefore* is followed by a comma.

1 Reread the text "Oceans." Find and underline the sentences with *therefore* and *that's why*. Notice the cause-and-effect relationship between each sentence you underlined and the sentence that comes before it.

2 Study the examples in the Language Focus box above. Then work with a partner. Match the effects in the right column below with the causes on the left. Make pairs of sentences using *therefore* and *that's why*.

Cause	**Effect (or Result)**
_____ **1** The five oceans flow into each other.	**a** He named the ocean *Mar Pacífico*, which means "peaceful ocean."
_____ **2** When Magellan first sailed on the Pacific, it was calm.	**b** From outer space, it looks as if Earth has one huge ocean.
_____ **3** In areas near the equator, there is a lot of evaporation and not a lot of rain.	**c** The place where the Amazon River empties into the Atlantic Ocean is less salty than the rest of the ocean.
_____ **4** Fresh river water dilutes the salt in ocean water.	**d** Ocean water near the equator usually has higher levels of salinity.

Task 5 IDENTIFYING CONCLUDING SENTENCES

> Remember that many paragraphs in academic English end with a
> **concluding sentence**, which restates the main idea of the paragraph in
> different words.

1 Look back at paragraph 1 of the text "Oceans." Label the concluding sentence (*CS*).
Compare the concluding sentence with the topic sentence.

2 Read the following paragraph. It is missing a concluding sentence.

> The Arctic and the Southern oceans differ in several ways. The Arctic Ocean
> is located at the North Pole, and it is surrounded by Canada, Norway, Greenland,
> Russia, and the United States. The Arctic Ocean is approximately 12 million
> square kilometers, and it is Earth's smallest ocean. It is also the coldest ocean.
> Its surface is often frozen in the winter, and much of its ice never melts. At the
> South Pole is the Southern Ocean, which surrounds Antarctica. The Southern
> Ocean is more than 20 million square kilometers and, therefore, larger than the
> Arctic Ocean. It is also warmer than the Arctic. Temperatures in the Southern
> Ocean range from -2° to 10°C (28° to 50°F), and strong winds often blow across
> its surface. In fact, the Southern Ocean is the windiest ocean on Earth. _____
> _____ .

Check (✔) the best concluding sentence for the paragraph above.

_____ **a** Therefore, the Arctic Ocean is smaller than the Southern Ocean.

_____ **b** Clearly, the Arctic and Southern oceans are important to life on our planet.

_____ **c** The facts clearly show that the Arctic and Southern oceans are different in
location, size, and weather.

3 Read the following paragraph. It is missing a concluding sentence. Write one.

> Jacques-Yves Cousteau (1910–1997) was a French explorer who
> dedicated his life to understanding and protecting the oceans. As a
> young man, Cousteau joined the French navy, and he began to do
> underwater research. He and an engineer, Emile Gagnan, created the
> aqualung. The aqualung is a piece of scuba-diving equipment that allows
> people to stay underwater for long periods of time. For more than 40
> years, Cousteau and his crew explored Earth's oceans and conducted
> research on his ship, the *Calypso*. He shared his knowledge and love of
> the oceans through his television films and books, and he helped people
> understand the need to protect this valuable resource. _____
> _____ .

Jacques-Yves Cousteau

Preparing to read

1 | The text you are going to read is about ocean currents. Read the following description of a current:

> A current is like a river of warm or cold water that flows through the ocean.

2 | Discuss the following questions in a small group:

1 What do you think causes ocean currents?
2 Do you know the names of any currents?
3 Why do you think currents are important?

EXAMINING GRAPHIC MATERIAL

Work with a partner. Look at Figure 4.1 on page 81. It shows several currents on the surface of the oceans. Mark the sentences below either *T* (true) or *F* (false), based on information on the map.

_____ 1 Near the equator, most currents flow from east to west.
_____ 2 Farther away from the equator, most currents flow from east to west.
_____ 3 In general, currents flow in a circle.
_____ 4 All currents are warm currents.
_____ 5 In the Atlantic Ocean, there is a warm current that flows along the east coast of North America.

Now read

Now read the text "Currents." When you finish, turn to the tasks on page 83.

2 CURRENTS

In May 1990, a cargo ship was traveling from Korea to the United States.   1
Soon after it left, a huge wave swept 21 containers of Nike shoes off the
ship and into the waters of the northern Pacific Ocean. Six months later,
people on the beaches of northern California, Oregon, Washington, and
British Columbia found hundreds of these shoes in the sand. Ocean currents had carried the shoes thousands of kilometers across the Pacific.

Surface currents and winds

A current is like a river of warm or cold water that flows through the   2
ocean. The currents in the top layer of the ocean (down to approximately
200 meters) are called surface currents, and they move in different
directions. The main cause of surface currents is wind. In general, surface currents in the ocean follow a circular path. They travel west along
the equator, turn as they reach a continent, travel east until they reach
another area of land, and then go west along the equator again. For
example, near the equator, there are winds called tropical trade winds.
Trade winds blow from east to west, and they create several currents
near the equator. These currents move in a westward direction. Between
the poles and the equator, there is another wind system, the westerlies.
These winds blow from west to east, creating currents that move in an
eastward direction.

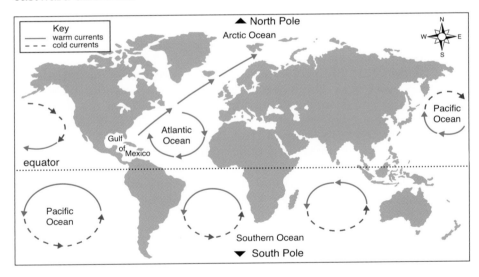

Figure 4.1 Major ocean currents

The role of surface currents

Surface currents help spread the heat from the sun around Earth. They   3
move water in big circles, so that cold water moves to warmer places,
and warm water moves to cooler places. This prevents, or stops, warm
water near the equator from becoming too hot. It also prevents cold
water near the North and South poles from becoming too cold.

Currents affect the temperature on land, as well as the temperature of water. The moving water of currents heats or cools the air around them. As a result, ocean currents can influence climate. A good example is the Gulf Stream. This huge warm-water current begins in the Gulf of Mexico, flows past the east coast of North America, and eventually reaches northern Europe. The warm water of the Gulf Stream causes parts of Ireland and England to have warmer temperatures than they normally would have.

4

Currents and climate change

Since ocean currents influence climate, changes in the way currents move can cause climate change. For example, thousands of years ago, the Gulf Stream stopped flowing. As a result, air temperatures in Europe decreased, and there was a small **ice age** until the Gulf Stream returned. Scientists tell us that similar changes in ocean currents could occur in the future. They continue to study the relationships between oceans and climates. This will help them better understand climate conditions today and changes that may come in the future.

5

ice age

a long period of time in which temperatures gradually decrease and thick sheets of ice cover large areas of land

Rip Currents

Rip currents are small currents that flow away from the shore out into the ocean. Unlike the Gulf Stream and other huge currents that travel for thousands of kilometers, rip currents flow only a few hundred meters. Although they are small, rip currents can be extremely dangerous because they travel very fast. A powerful rip can carry a swimmer too far out into the ocean in less than a minute.

More than 100 people drown in rip currents in the United States every year. This is often what happens: A swimmer feels that he or she is suddenly moving quickly away from the shore. The swimmer gets very nervous and tries to swim back to shore against the powerful current. This is extremely tiring. The swimmer becomes too tired to swim anymore and then drowns.

Rip currents occur at many beaches around the world. Here are some guidelines that will help keep you safe in the ocean:

- Swim only at beaches with lifeguards, and never swim alone.
- If you find yourself in a rip current, stay calm. Do not try to fight the current.
- Swim parallel to (go in the same direction as) the shore until you are out of the rip current.
- If that does not work, try to float and let the current carry you to its end. Then swim back to shore.

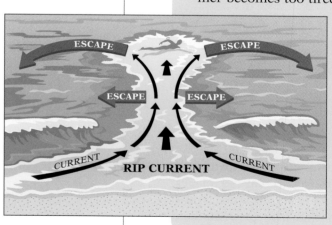

After you read

Task 1 HIGHLIGHTING KEY WORDS AND MAIN IDEAS

> Remember that highlighting is a helpful way to remember important information, such as the main ideas and key terms in a text.

1 Highlight the following key words in the text "Currents" and the boxed text "Rip Currents." Then use the information to write a definition for each word.

currents	Gulf Stream	rip currents	trade winds	westerlies

2 Read the questions below about the main ideas of the text. Find the sentence (or sentences) in the text that answers each question and highlight it. Use a different color from the one you used for the key words in step 1.

1 What causes surface currents?

2 What path do surface currents usually follow?

3 What do surface currents do?

4 How do currents affect water and land?

5 What is the name of a famous warm-water current? Where does it flow?

6 What are rip currents? Why are they dangerous?

Task 2 LABELING A MAP

1 On the map of ocean currents below, label the compass with the letters: *N* (north), *S* (south), *E* (east), *W* (west). Then label the following: *equator (EQ)*, *North Pole (NP)*, *South Pole (SP)*, *the westerlies (WS)*, *trade winds (TW)*, *Gulf Stream (GS)*.

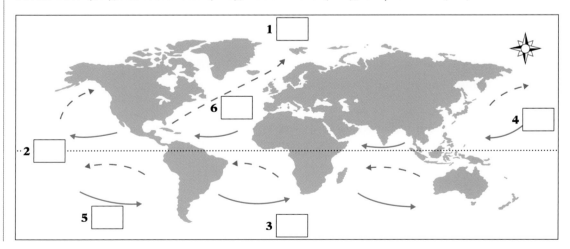

2 Look back at the text "Currents" and Figure 4.1 to check your work.

Task 3 LANGUAGE FOCUS: SUBJECT-VERB AGREEMENT

- In sentences beginning with *there is* or *there are*, the *be* verb agrees with the noun after it.

        singular form of *be*   singular noun

There   **is**   a warm **current**   off the coast of Alaska.

- If a subject has a prepositional phrase after it, the verb agrees with the subject of the sentence, not with the object of the preposition.

                   prepositional phrase

plural subject   object of the preposition   plural verb

Winds   near the equator   **blow**   from west to east.

Circle the correct forms of the verbs in parentheses. Compare your answers with a partner's.

1 There (is / are) a cold ocean current near the coast of California.
2 A warm current near the coast of Japan (flow / flows) from south to north.
3 Currents near the equator generally (travel / travels) in a westward direction.
4 The winds between the poles and the equator (blow / blows) from west to east.
5 There (is / are) winds called tropical trade winds near the equator.
6 Currents in the ocean (have / has) an effect on Earth's climates.

Task 4 LANGUAGE FOCUS: *TOO* AND *VERY*

You can use *too* or *very* before an adjective to give more detail about that adjective. *Too* before an adjective usually has a negative meaning. Use *too* to show that something is more than you need or more than you want.

    The water is **too** cold. We can't go swimming.

Use *very* to emphasize, or give importance to, an adjective.

    The water was **very** cold when we went swimming.

1 | Look back at the boxed text, "Rip Currents." Find and underline all the examples of *too* and *very*. Then take turns with a partner, and explain why the writer chose either *too* or *very* in each sentence.

2 | Choose either *too* or *very* to complete the following sentences.

1 The sun was (too / very) hot. We couldn't stay at the beach.
2 The rip currents were (too / very) strong. We didn't go in the water.
3 The swimmer was (too / very) calm. She swam parallel to the shore, out of the rip.
4 The waves were (too / very) big. It was a good day for surfing.
5 The waves were (too / very) big. The lifeguard told people to stay out of the water.

Task 5   WRITING ON TOPIC

After you write a paragraph once (first draft), read it again to make sure that all the sentences are on topic. Identify any irrelevant sentences, that is, sentences that do not support the topic, and cross them out. This will make the paragraph stronger and more focused. Then rewrite the paragraph (second draft).

1 Read the following paragraph. It has two irrelevant sentences. One is crossed out. Find the other sentence and cross it out.

One of the most important currents on Earth is the Antarctic Circumpolar Current. This current flows from west to east in the Southern Ocean. Strong westerly winds blow the current around the continent of Antarctica through the waters of the Atlantic, Pacific, and Indian Oceans. ~~These three oceans also have many other currents.~~ The Antarctic Circumpolar Current is the largest ocean current in the world, and it moves more water around the globe than any other current. It also keeps warm ocean water away from Antarctica. Ocean water is warm near the equator. That's why the ice there does not melt.

2 Read the following paragraph. Find and cross out two irrelevant sentences.

Like the Gulf Stream Current, the Humboldt Current has a strong effect on the climate of the land it flows past. This cold-water current travels south along the west coast of South America, from northern Peru to the southern end of Chile. Air temperatures in Chile are cooler than we would expect because of this ocean current. The California Current makes the climate of the Hawaiian Islands cooler than we might expect, too. The Humboldt Current also affects climate in another way: It makes areas of northern Chile, southern Peru, and Ecuador extremely dry. Peru and Ecuador are countries in South America.

3 Choose one of the paragraphs above and write a second draft. Make sure to delete the irrelevant sentences. Then add a concluding sentence to the paragraph.

Preparing to read

BRAINSTORMING

> Brainstorming is one way to find out how much you know about a topic before you read. When you brainstorm, try to think of as many ideas as you can about the topic. Do not try to organize your ideas or judge whether they are good or bad.

In a small group, brainstorm about how oceans influence people's lives. Try to think of all the ways (both good and bad) in which oceans affect us. Choose one person in your group to make a list of everyone's ideas.

BRAINSTORMING: ORGANIZING YOUR IDEAS

> After you brainstorm, it is useful to organize your ideas into categories. This will help you think, talk, and write about the ideas in a logical way.

In your group, organize the ideas you brainstormed. Use a chart like the one below.

How oceans influence our lives	Ideas from your brainstorming list
Good ways	
Bad ways	

Now read

Now read the text "Waves and Tsunamis." When you finish, turn to the tasks on page 89.

3 WAVES AND TSUNAMIS

The ocean can be beautiful and enjoyable. Many people like walking on
the beach and watching the water. Others enjoy swimming, surfing, and
sailing. However, the ocean is not predictable, and it can be very dangerous. Wind can create big waves that knock people down, sink boats,
and damage the shoreline. Giant waves, called tsunamis, can kill people
and wash away entire towns. The ocean is truly a place of great beauty
and great danger.

1

Wind and waves

In addition to causing currents, the wind creates waves as it blows
across the surface of the ocean. The stronger the wind is, the bigger the
waves are. You may have been at the beach on a windy day when big
waves crashed onto the shore. If you were at the beach on a calm, wind-
less day, you probably noticed the flat surface of the water.

2

Scientists measure waves from their highest point, the crest, to their
lowest point, the trough. Most waves are neither very big nor dangerous. However, some waves, such as those in a violent storm, are large
enough to damage ships and hurt people on the shore. Careful swim-
mers and surfers do not go into the ocean if the waves are too big, and
ship captains often change direction to stay away from a storm. The
power of the wind and the waves can be deadly.

3

Tsunamis

The biggest, most powerful waves on our planet, called tsunamis, are
not caused by the wind. Tsunamis form when an underwater volcano
erupts or an earthquake occurs on the ocean floor. Tsunamis move very
quickly across the open ocean, sometimes more than 800 kilometers an
hour, as fast as an airplane. In the deep ocean, tsunamis do not look like

4

giant waves. In fact, they are usually less than one meter high. However, as they approach land and move into shallow water, they are forced to slow down. This causes the waves to suddenly rise up high in the air and then slam down on the land. In shallow coastal waters, tsunamis can cause waves to rise more than 30 meters high and cause terrible damage to the coast, killing people and destroying buildings and crops.

A tsunami wave breaking near Monterey, California

In 1960, a huge earthquake occurred off the coast of Chile. Fifteen minutes later, a tsunami hit the Chilean coast. Fifteen hours later, another tsunami hit Hilo, Hawaii. Seven hours later, another tsunami hit Japan. Thousands of people died because of the tsunamis that occurred after the Chilean earthquake. However, the deadliest series of tsunamis happened on December 26, 2004, when a powerful earthquake occurred in the Indian Ocean. The earthquake caused tsunamis that hit a dozen countries, including Indonesia, India, Sri Lanka, and Thailand. The tsunamis killed more than 250,000 people and destroyed hundreds of towns.

5

The next time you go to the beach, take a few moments to appreciate both the beauty and the danger of the ocean. Never forget what the power of the waves can do.

6

Surviving the 2004 Tsunami

On December 26, 2004, most people had no warning that tsunamis were moving across the Indian Ocean and would soon reach land. As a result, thousands of people died. However, on the Indian island of South Andaman, one group of people, the Jarawa tribe, seemed to know that a tsunami was coming. The Jarawa is one of the oldest tribes on earth, perhaps 70,000 years old. All 250 members of the tribe escaped safely from the coast to the jungle before the tsunami arrived, and they stayed there for several days. The Jarawa people do not like to talk to people outside their tribe. That's why they have not explained how they knew the tsunami was coming. However, some scientists think they have an explanation. They believe it was the Jawaras' knowledge of the movements of the ocean, the earth, and the wind, and the behavior of the birds that helped this ancient tribe predict the tsunami and survive.

After you read

Task 1   READING FOR MAIN IDEAS AND DETAILS

Read each sentence below and decide if it is a main idea or a detail in the "Waves and Tsunamis" text. Write the correct letter in the blank next to each sentence. (Hint: There are three main ideas in the list.)

M = a main idea in the text
D = a detail in the text

_____ **1** The wind creates waves as it blows across the surface of the ocean.

_____ **2** On windy days, big waves crash onto the shore.

_____ **3** Storm waves can damage ships and hurt people.

_____ **4** Tsunamis are the biggest waves on our planet, and they can cause terrible damage.

_____ **5** Tsunamis can travel 800 kilometers per hour.

_____ **6** The deadliest series of tsunamis happened on December 26, 2004.

_____ **7** The ocean is both beautiful and dangerous.

_____ **8** Tsunamis rise high in the air as they approach land.

Task 2   BUILDING VOCABULARY: ADJECTIVE SUFFIXES

You can change many nouns and verbs into adjectives by adding suffixes such as *-ful*, *-able*, and *-ous*. Some words are both nouns and verbs. Look at these examples:

Noun and/or verb	Adjective
truth (*n.*)	truthful
prevent (*v.*)	preventable
love (*n., v.*)	lovable
mountain (*n.*)	mountainous

1   Read the list of nouns and verbs in the left column below. Find and circle the adjective forms of these words in the text "Waves and Tsunamis." Then write each adjective next to the appropriate word below.

Adjective form

1 beauty (*n.*)   _____ (par. 1)

2 enjoy (*v.*)   _____ (par. 1)

3 predict (*v.*)   _____ (par. 1)

4 danger (*n.*)   _____ (par. 1)

5 care (*n., v.*)   _____ (par. 3)

2 Fill in the blanks in the following sentences with the adjectives from step 1.

    1 Swimming at the beach on a sunny day can be very _____.

    2 It is very _____ to be on the beach when a tsunami reaches land.

    3 A _____ swimmer never goes swimming alone.

    4 Earthquakes are not _____, but there are things you can do to prepare for them.

    5 Last night, the sunset over the ocean was very _____.

3 Work with a partner. On a separate piece of paper, write four or five sentences, using the adjectives in steps 1 and 2.

Task 3   LANGUAGE FOCUS: PARALLEL STRUCTURE

In a sentence with a conjunction such as *and*, the words or phrases before and after the conjunction must have the same part of speech. This creates parallel structure in the sentence.

Look at these examples:

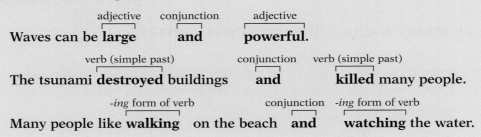

1 Reread paragraph 1 of the text "Waves and Tsunamis." Find and underline five examples of parallel structure. Then compare your answers with a partner's.

2 In each sentence below, find the error in parallel structure. First, find *and*. Then make sure the parts of speech before and after *and* are the same. Write the correct sentences on a separate piece of paper. Look back at the text to check your answers.

    1 The ocean can be beautiful and enjoyment.

    2 Many people like walking on the beach and to watch the water.

    3 The wind can create big waves that knock people down, sink boats, and damaged the shoreline.

    4 The power of the windy and the waves can be deadly.

    5 The tsunamis killed more than 250,000 people and destroying hundreds of towns.

Task 4 LANGUAGE FOCUS: *BOTH . . . AND* AND *NEITHER . . . NOR*

Both . . . and and *neither . . . nor* are two-part conjunctions that require parallel structure. In other words, the parts of speech that follow each conjunction must be the same. Look at these examples:

      conjunction adjective conjunction adjective

The Great Lakes are both deep and   wide.

 conjunction noun conjunction noun

Neither lakes nor rivers are as salty as oceans.

1 Look back at the text "Waves and Tsunamis." With a partner, find and underline sentences in the text with *both . . . and* and *neither . . . nor*. How many did you find? Which words have the same form in each sentence?

2 Complete each sentence below with a word from the box. Make sure each sentence has parallel structure.

dangerous	preventable	Southern	volcanoes	waves

1 Wind creates both currents and _____.

2 The Pacific Ocean is violent because it has both earthquakes and _____.

3 Neither the Arctic nor the _____ Ocean is as large as the Atlantic.

4 Earthquakes are neither predictable nor _____.

5 The ocean is both enjoyable and _____.

Task 5 WRITING THE SECOND DRAFT OF A PARAGRAPH

Read the incomplete paragraph below. Complete the topic sentence, add a concluding sentence, and cross out the irrelevant sentence. Then write a second draft of the paragraph on a separate piece of paper.

> Duke Kahanamoku _____
> _____. He was born in 1890 in Honolulu, Hawaii, and he spent his whole life near the ocean. Although Kahanamoku enjoyed swimming and canoeing, he was most famous for his skill in surfing. In fact, many people consider him the father of surfing. He traveled frequently and introduced surfing to people all over the world. He won five Olympic medals in swimming. When Kahanamoku was born, very few people surfed. By the time he died, surfing was a sport that millions of people enjoyed. _____
> _____.

Duke Kahanamoku

Chapter 4   Writing Assignment

Write a paragraph about one of the oceans on Earth. For example, you could write about the ocean's location and size, history, or special features. Use information from this chapter and your own ideas. Find some additional information in the library or on the Internet. Follow the steps and the guidelines below.

1 Choose one ocean and find some information about it. Take notes on what you find.

2 In a small group, share what you learned about the ocean you chose.

3 Then, on your own, choose two or three important ideas that you want to include in your paragraph. Think of at least one detail or example to support each idea.

4 Now write the first draft of the paragraph.

   1 Write a topic sentence that states the main idea of the paragraph.
   2 Write four to six supporting sentences based on the ideas, details, and examples you chose in step 3.
   3 End the paragraph with a concluding sentence that restates the main idea. (Be sure to make the concluding sentence a little different from the topic sentence.)
   4 Give your paragraph a title.

Guidelines

- Use correct paragraph form and structure.
- Try to include some of the vocabulary you learned in this chapter.
- Make sure the subject and verb in each sentence agree with each other.
- Try to include some of the forms and structures you learned in this chapter, such as superlative adjectives (see the Language Focus task, page 77), *therefore* and *that's why* (see the Language Focus task, page 78), and parallel structure (see the Language Focus tasks, pages 90–91).

---

5 When you finish writing, exchange paragraphs with a partner and read each other's work. Then discuss the following questions about both paragraphs:

   1 Which idea in your partner's paragraph do you think is the most interesting?
   2 Does your partner's paragraph have a topic sentence that states the main idea?
   3 Are all the supporting sentences on topic? Are there any irrelevant sentences?
   4 Does the paragraph have a concluding sentence that restates the main idea?

6 Think about any changes to your paragraph that would improve it. Then write a second draft of the paragraph.

The Air Around Us

In this unit, we look at the air that surrounds our planet and its weather. In Chapter 5, we examine what Earth's atmosphere is made of, why it is important, and its structure. We also discuss clouds. In Chapter 6, we focus on weather conditions in the atmosphere. We look at different climates around the world, climate change, and several types of storms.

Previewing the unit

Read the contents page for Unit 3, and do the following activities.

Chapter 5: Earth's Atmosphere

In this chapter, you are going to explore Earth's atmosphere.

1| Work with a partner. Go outside, or open a window. Then discuss the questions below and take notes on your answers.

   1 Take a deep breath of air. The air is part of our planet's atmosphere. Can you see the atmosphere? Can you smell it or feel it? Do you think the atmosphere is the same everywhere?

   2 Next, look up into the air. What do you see? For example, do you see any birds? Make a list of all the things you can see in the atmosphere.

   3 There are some things in the air that you cannot see, such as rockets that carry astronauts far beyond Earth. Name some other things in the air that you cannot see, and add them to the list.

   4 Do you see any clouds in the air? What can clouds tell us about the weather?

2| Discuss the results of your activities in step 1 in a small group or as a class.

Chapter 6: Weather and Climate

This chapter discusses Earth's weather and climate, or long-term weather conditions.

1| When people describe the weather, they talk about things like air temperature, wind, and rain or snow. In a small group, describe what the weather is usually like in the place where you grew up. Did you and your classmates grow up in similar or different climates?

2| Storms are an important part of weather conditions. Read the names of the storms below. Check (✔) the storms that are common in places you have lived.

   _____ rainstorms   _____ hurricanes

   _____ snowstorms   _____ tornadoes

   _____ thunderstorms

3| In your group, talk about big storms that you remember.

4| Which type of storm do you think is the most common on our planet? Which one do you think is the most deadly?

Unit Contents 3

Preparing to read

BUILDING BACKGROUND KNOWLEDGE ABOUT THE TOPIC

1 | You are going to read a text titled "The Composition of the Atmosphere." The atmosphere is one of Earth's four systems. What do you think *composition* means? Look up the word in a dictionary if you do not know the meaning.

2 | Read the following sentences from the text and answer the questions below with a partner.

> The atmosphere is a blanket of gases that covers every part of our planet Earth. It is the air around us.

1 What is the atmosphere?

2 The atmosphere is composed of 12 different gases. Do you know the names of any gases in the atmosphere? If so, name the ones you know.

3 | We often use chemical symbols to represent gases. For example, the symbol for argon, a gas, is Ar. Below is a list of six gases in the atmosphere. With your partner, try to match each gas on the left with its symbol on the right. Then check your answers at the bottom of the page.

_____	**1** hydrogen	**a**	O_3
_____	**2** oxygen	**b**	CO_2
_____	**3** nitrogen	**c**	He
_____	**4** ozone	**d**	H
_____	**5** helium	**e**	N
_____	**6** carbon dioxide	**f**	O

4 | Two of the gases in the list make up most of Earth's atmosphere. Can you guess which ones they are?

Now read

Now read the text "The Composition of the Atmosphere." When you finish, turn to the tasks on page 99.

Answers to step 3: 1 d, 2 f, 3 e, 4 a, 5 c, 6 b

Earth's Atmosphere

1 THE COMPOSITION OF THE ATMOSPHERE

The atmosphere is a blanket of gases that covers every part of our planet Earth. It is the air around us. You cannot see air, but you can feel it when the wind blows. Every time you take a breath, you take it into your lungs.

1

What is it that goes into your lungs when you breathe? Our air is composed of a mixture of 12 gases: nitrogen, oxygen, argon, carbon dioxide, water vapor, neon, helium, methane, krypton, hydrogen, ozone, and xenon. The two main gases are nitrogen and oxygen. The atmosphere consists of 78 percent nitrogen and 21 percent oxygen. Although the other gases make up only a small percentage of the atmosphere, they are very important.

2

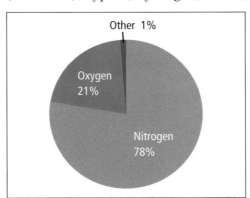

Figure 5.1 The gases in Earth's atmosphere

Humans need the atmosphere for many reasons. First, our bodies need the oxygen in the air to keep us alive. Second, the nitrogen in the air is necessary for the plants that we grow for food. In addition, the atmosphere acts like a shield around Earth. It protects us from objects that fall from space, such as **meteors**. The ozone in the atmosphere also provides protection by blocking harmful rays from the sun, which would burn us. Finally, some gases help control temperatures on Earth. Carbon dioxide, for example, keeps the air from becoming too cold. It is the special combination of gases in the atmosphere that allows life on Earth to exist.

meteor

a piece of rock or metal from outer space that makes a bright light in the sky as it falls into Earth's atmosphere

Oxygen

Oxygen is one of the main gases in Earth's atmosphere. Its chemical symbol is O. Oxygen has no color, odor, or taste, but our world could not exist without it. Oxygen makes up 21 percent of Earth's atmosphere, almost 90 percent of the water in our oceans, nearly 50 percent of Earth's crust, and about 60 percent of the human body. Almost all living things need oxygen for life.

Oxygen also has several other important uses. For example, it is used in the production of steel, plastics, and textiles, such as cotton and silk. Liquid oxygen is used to make fuel for space rockets. In hospitals, doctors give pure oxygen to patients with breathing problems. Oxygen can also be mixed with other gases to help people breathe more easily in high-flying planes and spacecraft. These vehicles travel high up in the atmosphere where there is less oxygen.

Oxygen even provides recreation for people who enjoy going to oxygen bars. These bars first appeared in Japan in the late 1990s, and now they can be found in other parts of the world. For about $1US a minute, customers can breathe air that has more oxygen than the usual 21 percent in the atmosphere. Customers at oxygen bars say that breathing this oxygen improves energy and lowers stress. However, scientific studies have not proven any of these benefits.

Customers at Thailand's first oxygen bar

After you read

Task 1   TEST TAKING: EXAMINING THE LANGUAGE OF TEST QUESTIONS

> When you answer test questions about a text, it is important to understand that the language (the words and phrases) in the questions may not be exactly the same as the language in the text.

1 | Answer the following questions with information from the text "The Composition of the Atmosphere."

   1 How many gases combine to create the atmosphere?

   2 Which are the two most common gases?

   3 Which gas helps plants?

   4 Which gas helps keeps us safe from the sun?

   5 Which gas prevents the air from becoming too cold?

   6 What makes life on Earth possible?

2 | Work with a partner. Look back at the text and underline the words and phrases that give the answers to the questions in step 1. Discuss the differences between the language in the questions and the language in the text.

Task 2   BUILDING VOCABULARY: USING CONTEXT TO GUESS NEW WORDS

> The context of a new word, that is, the words and phrases that surround it, can often help you guess the meaning.

Look at the words in the left column below and then find them in the text "The Composition of the Atmosphere." Use the context of each word to help you match it with its definition.

_____ **1** blanket

_____ **2** lungs

_____ **3** shield

_____ **4** meteor

_____ **5** rays

a beams of light from the sun

b something that covers something else to protect it from harm or damage

c the parts of the body that help a person breathe

d a layer that covers something

e a piece of rock or metal that produces a bright light when it falls from space into Earth's atmosphere

Task 3 LANGUAGE FOCUS: EXPRESSING PARTS

> Here are some ways to express that something has several parts:
>
> X **is composed of** A, B, and C.
> X **consists of** A, B, and C.
> A, B, and C **make up** X.

1 | Find and circle three different ways of expressing parts in the text "The Composition of the Atmosphere."

2 | Complete the sentences below about the composition of the atmosphere. Base your answers on information in the text, Figure 5.1 on page 97, and the boxed text on page 98. Fill in each blank with one word.

1 Earth's _____ consists _____ 78 percent _____ and _____ percent oxygen.

2 Ten gases _____ _____ less than one _____ of the atmosphere.

3 The _____ is _____ of 12 _____.

4 The atmosphere _____ _____ several gases that are essential for human life.

5 Oxygen _____ _____ almost _____ percent of Earth's crust.

6 The atmosphere _____ of less than _____ _____ carbon dioxide.

Task 4 REVIEWING PARAGRAPH STRUCTURE

> Remember that many paragraphs in academic writing have the following structure:
>
> • The **topic sentence** is usually the first sentence. It tells readers the main idea of the paragraph, with no details.
> • **Supporting sentences** follow the topic sentence. They provide specific details and examples to show that the topic sentence is true. They also explain the topic sentence more fully.
> • The **concluding sentence** is the last sentence. It repeats the main idea of the paragraph, but it is not a copy of the topic sentence.

Look back at the text "The Composition of the Atmosphere." Find the paragraph that has a structure like the one described in the box above. Put a check (✔) next to it. Compare your answers with a partner's.

Task 5 ORGANIZING IDEAS WITH TRANSITION WORDS

It is important to organize ideas in your writing so that a reader can understand them. After you write the topic sentence, consider how to present the supporting sentences in a logical way and how to connect them to each other. You can connect sentences by using one of the following transition words:

First,
Second,
In addition,
. . . also . . .
Finally,

1 The sentences below are from paragraph 3 of the text "The Composition of the Atmosphere." Number the sentences in order (1–8) without looking back at the text. Use the transition words in the sentences to help you.

_____ **a** In addition, the atmosphere acts like a shield around Earth.

_____ **b** It is the special combination of gases in the atmosphere that allows life on Earth to exist.

_____ **c** Second, the nitrogen in the air is necessary for the plants that we grow for food.

_____ **d** Humans need the atmosphere for many reasons.

_____ **e** First, our bodies need the oxygen in the air to keep us alive.

_____ **f** Finally, some gases help control temperatures on Earth.

_____ **g** It protects us from objects that fall from space, such as meteors.

_____ **h** The ozone in the atmosphere also provides protection by blocking harmful rays from the sun, which would burn us.

2 Use information from the text "The Composition of the Atmosphere" and Figure 5.1 on page 97 to write a paragraph about some of the gases in the air. Do not copy sentences from the text. Follow these steps:

1 Write a topic sentence to begin your paragraph. Remember that the topic sentence states the main idea, without details.

2 Choose two or three gases. Write one or more details about each gas in the supporting sentences of your paragraph. Use transition words to organize the sentences.

3 End with a concluding sentence that restates the main idea of the paragraph.

4 Compare your paragraph with a partner's.

Preparing to read

PREVIEWING KEY PARTS OF A TEXT

Remember that previewing key parts of a text before you read it will help you understand the main ideas.

Preview the title, the introductory paragraph (par. 1), and the headings in the text on pages 103–104 to get a general idea of what it is about. Then answer the following questions with a partner:

1 What do you think the text is about?

2 How many layers does the atmosphere have?

EXAMINING GRAPHIC MATERIAL

Look at Figure 5.2 on page 103. Then answer the following questions in a small group:

1 What is the name of the bottom layer of the atmosphere?

2 What is the name of the top layer of the atmosphere?

3 Which layer is the largest?

4 In which layers do airplanes fly?

5 In which layer of the atmosphere do satellites orbit Earth?

6 Which layer contains living things?

Now read

Now read the text "The Structure of the Atmosphere." When you finish, turn to the tasks on page 105.

2 THE STRUCTURE OF THE ATMOSPHERE

The atmosphere around Earth extends far above its surface. There is no definite boundary, or line, where the atmosphere ends. The air just gets thinner and thinner. In other words, the upper atmosphere has less oxygen, and it eventually blends into space. Scientists divide the atmosphere into five layers: the troposphere, the stratosphere, the mesosphere, the thermosphere, and the exosphere.

The troposphere

The troposphere is the first layer of the atmosphere. It extends from Earth's surface to an average of 12 kilometers above the surface. There is a lot of movement and activity in this layer. It contains all the familiar parts of our world: the oceans, the mountains, the clouds, and all living things. Because most of the water in the atmosphere is located here, it is where weather conditions, such as rain, snow, and thunder, occur. In addition, the air in the troposphere is always moving. The movement creates turbulence, a very unstable flow of air.

The stratosphere

The second layer of the atmosphere is the stratosphere. It starts at 12 kilometers and ends at about 50 kilometers above Earth. There is no wind or weather in the stratosphere, and there are few clouds. The air is very stable (still) and clear. As a result, pilots sometimes fly there, above the troposphere, to enjoy a smooth ride. It is in the stratosphere that we find the ozone layer. The ozone layer is very important because it absorbs dangerous ultraviolet radiation, or invisible rays of energy that are sent out from the sun. Without it, humans and animals would probably die from the sun's radiation.

The mesosphere

About 50 kilometers above Earth, the stratosphere ends and the mesosphere begins. It extends from 50 kilometers to 80 kilometers above the surface. The air in this layer becomes very thin, and the temperature drops to as low as -93° Celsius. In fact, the mesosphere is the coldest layer of the atmosphere. Most people will never go to the mesosphere, but sometimes we can see what happens there. Every day millions of meteors enter our

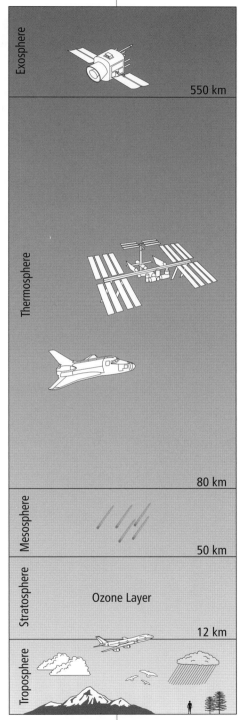

Figure 5.2 The layers of the atmosphere

atmosphere from outer space, and they burn up in the mesosphere. Sometimes we can see them as shooting stars in the night sky.

The thermosphere

The fourth layer of the atmosphere is the thermosphere, which is located approximately 80 kilometers above Earth's surface. In this layer, the temperature starts to increase again. In fact, the thermosphere is the hottest layer of the atmosphere. The only humans who have ever traveled here are astronauts as they orbit Earth on a space shuttle or other spacecraft. The **International Space Station** also orbits Earth in the thermosphere.

5

The exosphere

Finally, approximately 550 kilometers above Earth, we reach the exosphere, the last layer of the atmosphere. At the edge of the exosphere, the air becomes extremely thin. Is there any sign of human life this high up? Yes. Thousands of man-made **satellites** orbit Earth in this layer.

6

The next time you look up at the sky, remember this: Each layer of the atmosphere is important. Together the layers produce breathable air, water, and protection from harmful things in space. As far as we know, Earth is the only planet with atmospheric layers that can support life.

7

International Space Station

a structure in space that many countries are building together to support space research

satellite (man-made)

an object that goes into space to collect information or to become part of a communications system

NASA and the Space Shuttle

In 1958, the United States formed an agency called NASA (National Aeronautics and Space Administration) to explore space. NASA began to launch, or send, satellites and rockets carrying humans high up into the atmosphere. In one 1969 NASA project, the astronaut Neil Armstrong became the first person to walk on the moon.

In 1981, NASA launched the first space shuttle. The space shuttle has an unusual shape, and it is the world's first spacecraft that can fly back and forth between Earth and space. NASA describes it this way: "It has the ability to take off like a rocket, orbit the Earth like a spaceship, and land on a runway like an airplane." In recent years, five different shuttles have made more than 100 flights into space.

Sadly, there were two terrible accidents in space shuttle history. *Challenger* (1986) and *Columbia* (2003) exploded, and all the astronauts onboard were killed. However, there have been successful shuttle flights since then. Astronauts on shuttles have launched and repaired satellites, studied the effects of space travel on humans, and contributed to the building of the International Space Station.

The crew of the space shuttle *Discovery*

After you read

Task 1 NOTE TAKING: USING A CHART

Putting your notes into chart form shows the information in a way that is easy to remember. A chart can also help you review information quickly for a test.

1 | The chart below shows the beginning of a student's notes on the text "The Structure of the Atmosphere." Complete the chart with information from the text. In the last column, try to write two pieces of information for each layer of Earth's atmosphere.

Layer	Name	Height (from ____ to ____)	Special features
1			• •
2		from 12 km to ____ km	• •
3	mesosphere		• •
4			• •
5		from ____ km to ?	• satellites in this layer •

2 | Compare your chart with a partner's.

Task 2 BUILDING VOCABULARY: HAVING FUN WITH WORDS

Thinking about word similarities and differences is a good way to develop your knowledge and understanding of words. You can play games with words to help you learn and remember them.

This game is called Odd One Out. In each row below, one of the words does not belong with the others. Work with a partner. Decide which word in each row does not belong and explain why.

1 shuttle   bird   satellite   plane
2 shuttle   bird   satellite   tree
3 shuttle   bird   cloud   tree
4 shuttle   pilot   astronaut   space station
5 rain   snow   cloud   thunder
6 atmosphere   exosphere   mesosphere   stratosphere

Task 3 PUNCTUATION: COLONS, *SUCH AS*, AND LISTS

Knowing how punctuation works can help you understand what you read. Look at these guidelines:

- Use a colon to introduce a complete list.

  The air is composed of a mixture of 12 different gases: **nitrogen, oxygen, argon, carbon dioxide, water vapor, neon, helium, methane, krypton, hydrogen, ozone, and xenon.**

- When a list is not complete, use *such as*. Notice that there is a comma before *such as*. It is not followed by a colon.

  The air is composed of a mixture of many different gases, **such as nitrogen, oxygen, argon, neon, and helium.**

Notice that in lists of more than two items, there is a comma after each item.

1 | Look back at paragraphs 1 and 2 of the text "The Structure of the Atmosphere." Find and underline three lists of items: two lists that follow a colon and one list that follows *such as*.

2 | The sentences below have incorrect punctuation. With a partner, discuss why each sentence is incorrect. Then, on your own, rewrite each sentence correctly.

   1 There are four main types of wet weather: rain, snow, hail, sleet.
   There are four main types of wet weather: rain, snow, hail, and sleet.

   2 There are several types of wet weather such as: rain, snow, and hail.

   _____

   3 There are four main types of wet weather: rain, snow, and hail, and sleet.

   _____

   4 There are several types of wet weather such as rain, snow, and hail.

   _____

   5 There are several types of wet weather, rain, snow, and hail.

   _____

   6 There are several types of wet weather such as, rain and, snow and, hail.

   _____

3 | Compare your sentences with a partner's.

Task 4 LANGUAGE FOCUS: EXPRESSING HEIGHT

Here are some structures you can use to express how high something is, including its location and range:

- **A is located X above B.**
  The exosphere **is located** 550 kilometers **above** Earth's surface.

- **A extends from X to Y above B.**
  The mesosphere **extends from** 50 kilometers **to** 80 kilometers **above** Earth.

- **A starts / begins at X and ends at Y above B.**
  The thermosphere **starts at** approximately 80 kilometers **and ends at** 550 kilometers **above** Earth.

1 Find and underline the expressions of height in the text "The Structure of the Atmosphere." Compare your answers with a partner's.

2 Use the structures in the box to complete the sentences below about the layers of the atmosphere. Fill in each blank with one word or number. You can look back at the text and Figure 5.2 to check information.

  1 The _____ extends _____ our planet's surface _____ an average of 12 kilometers above the surface.

  2 The _____ is located 30 kilometers above the stratosphere.

  3 The mesosphere _____ at 50 kilometers and _____ _____ 80 kilometers above Earth.

  4 The thermosphere _____ located _____ kilometers _____ Earth.

  5 Satellites _____ _____ hundreds of kilometers above Earth in the _____ .

3 Now write two sentences of your own about the layers of the atmosphere. Use an expression of height in each sentence.

Task 5 USING EXPRESSIONS OF HEIGHT

Write a paragraph about the layers of the atmosphere. Follow these steps:

  1 Start the paragraph with this topic sentence: Earth's atmosphere consists of five layers.

  2 Write two or three supporting sentences about each layer. Include some expressions of height and a few interesting facts. You may use information from your chart from the Note Taking task on page 105, but do not copy sentences from the text.

  3 Write a concluding sentence to end the paragraph. Remember that it should not be a copy of the topic sentence.

Preparing to read

BUILDING BACKGROUND KNOWLEDGE ABOUT THE TOPIC

Look at the three pictures of clouds. Then work with a partner to answer the questions below.

a

b

c

1 Do you know the names of the clouds in the pictures? Do you know the names of any other clouds? Name the clouds you know.

2 What is the weather usually like when you see each of the clouds? What kind of weather do you expect to come soon? Use the words in the box to help you talk about the weather.

bad weather	blue sky	cold	fog	good weather	ice
rain	snow	stormy	sunny	warm	wet

3 Study the pictures below. They show the three forms (states) of matter that water can take.

 **liquid**

 **solid**

gas

4 Complete the sentences below. Write *gas*, *liquid*, or *solid* to describe the different states of matter that water can take in Earth's atmosphere.

1 Water in ice takes the form of a _____.

2 Water in rain drops takes the form of a _____.

3 Water that is neither a liquid nor a solid is a _____. (It is called water vapor.)

Now read

Now read the text "Clouds." When you finish, turn to the tasks on page 111.

3 CLOUDS

Clouds are a familiar sight in the troposphere. Have you ever wondered what they are made of? Clouds are composed of billions of tiny water droplets or ice crystals. To understand how clouds form, consider this special feature of water: It can change from a gas (vapor) to a liquid (water) to a solid (ice) and back again. Clouds form when warm water vapor in the air rises in the atmosphere. The air cools and then becomes tiny drops of water or ice. These droplets of water or ice join together in the sky and form clouds. Although clouds come in many different shapes and sizes, there are three main types: cumulus, cirrus, and stratus.

Cumulus clouds

Cumulus clouds are fluffy white clouds. They look like balls of cotton in the sky. This is the type of cloud that you often see in a child's drawing. When you see cumulus clouds, the weather is generally good, and the sky is blue. Cumulus clouds are low-level clouds. They are usually close to the ground, at about 460 to 915 meters above Earth's surface. A cumulus cloud forms when sunshine warms water vapor in the air. The warm water vapor rises and cools as it moves higher. The cool water vapor then changes into water droplets that join together and form a cumulus cloud.

Cumulus clouds

Cirrus clouds

Cirrus clouds are thin, wispy white clouds. They look like the tail of a horse or a curl of hair. When you see cirrus clouds in the sky, it usually means that stormy weather is on its way. Cirrus clouds are located very high in the sky, about 5 to 15 kilometers above the ground in the troposphere. Because it is very cold high in the troposphere, cirrus clouds are made up of tiny ice crystals, not water droplets. A cirrus cloud forms when cold air moves under an area of warm air and pushes the warm air higher in the troposphere. The warm air cools, changes into ice crystals, and a cirrus cloud forms.

Cirrus clouds

Stratus clouds

Stratus clouds

Stratus clouds look like gray, shapeless blankets covering most of the sky. They are usually only about 0.8 kilometers thick, but they can be almost 1,000 kilometers wide. When you see stratus clouds, you might soon see rain. Stratus clouds are low-level clouds, located quite close to the ground. In fact, sometimes they lie on the ground or the ocean, and then they are called fog. A stratus cloud forms when warm, wet air moves slowly over an area of cooler air. The warm air rises, cools, and changes into water droplets. The droplets join together and create a stratus cloud.

There are many other types of clouds. Each one forms in a different way, and each one can tell you something about the coming weather. If you pay careful attention to the types of clouds in the sky, you can predict the weather fairly accurately.

Figure 5.3 Common types of clouds in the troposphere

The Latin Origin of Cloud Names

Scientists often use Greek or Latin words to name plants, animals, and other things in nature. Cloud names come from the Latin language. *Cumulus* is the Latin word for a large heap or lump. *Cirrus* means "curl" in Latin, and *stratus* refers to a blanket or layer. *Cumulus*, *cirrus*, and *stratus* can also combine with other Latin words. For example, *nimbus* means "rain" or "storm," so cumulonimbus clouds are big heaps of rain clouds. Another example is *alto*. Although *alto* means "high," scientists use this prefix to describe mid-level clouds. For instance, altostratus clouds are layers of clouds that are neither very high nor very low in the sky. After you learn the Latin words, you will be able to understand the name of almost every cloud in the sky.

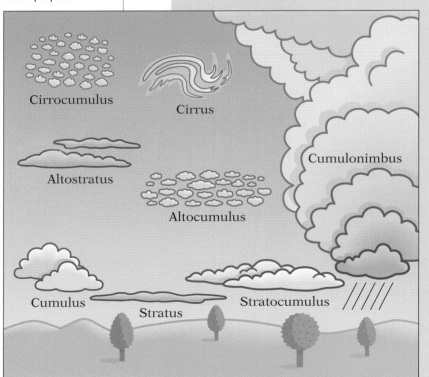

Cirrocumulus

Cirrus

Altostratus

Altocumulus

Cumulonimbus

Cumulus

Stratus

Stratocumulus

After you read

Task 1 NOTE TAKING: USING A CHART

The chart below shows the beginning of a student's notes on the text "Clouds." Copy the chart on a separate piece of paper, and fill in the missing information. In the last column, draw a picture of each type of cloud.

Cloud name	Description	Picture
Cumulus		
	• thin, wispy, white • looks like a thin curl of hair • found 5–15 km above ground	

Task 2 NOTE TAKING: USING SYMBOLS AND ABBREVIATIONS

When you take notes on a text, try to abbreviate (shorten) words and use symbols to represent words when you can. This will help you take notes more quickly. Below are examples of some common abbreviations and symbols. You can also create your own to make your notes especially meaningful to you.

Abbreviation		**Symbol**	
m	*meters*	&	*and*
@	*at*	≈	*approximately*
b/c	*because*	→	*causes* or *leads to*

1 Work with a partner. Guess the meanings of the symbols and abbreviations below. Then add three more to the list.

   a info _____   **d** + _____   **g** ___ _____

   b ex _____   **e** ↑ _____   **h** ___ _____

   c km _____   **f** = _____   **i** ___ _____

2 Share your answers with your classmates.

3 Below are some notes on a paragraph in the text "Clouds." Work with a partner. Take turns using the notes to make sentences about cumulus clouds.

Cumulus clouds
- *fluffy & white*
- *usually = good weather*
- *low level (≈ 460–915 m above ground)*
- *sun warms water vapor → water vapor rises → water vapor cools → water droplets = cumulus clouds*

4 Complete these notes on the paragraph about cirrus clouds.

Cirrus clouds
- *thin, wispy, white*
- *usually = _____ soon*
- *high level (_____)*
- *b/c cold @ high level, made of ice, not _____*
- *cold air moves under warm air → warm air _____*
- *→ warm air cools → _____ = _____*

5 Now write your own notes on the paragraph about stratus clouds.

Task 3 BUILDING VOCABULARY: WORDS FROM LATIN AND GREEK

Remember that many scientific words come from Latin or Greek.

1 Reread the boxed text "The Latin Origin of Cloud Names" on page 110. Below are the names of two more types of clouds. Use the information in the boxed text to guess what these clouds look like.

1 nimbostratus
2 cirrostratus

2 Draw a picture of each cloud in step 1. Compare your drawings with a partner's.

3 Look at the following list of word parts from Greek and Latin and their meanings.

astro-	star	*-graph*	write, written	*photo-*	light
bio-	life	*-logy*	study	*-scope*	observe, see
geo-	earth, rock	*-meter*	measure	*tele-*	far, distant

4 Work with a partner and guess the meanings of the following words. Then check your answers in a dictionary.

a telescope   **c** astrometry   **e** biology   **g** telephoto

b geology   **d** biometrics   **f** astrophotography   **h** photometer

5 What other words in English can you make from the words in the box? Share them with the class.

Task 4   LANGUAGE FOCUS: *WHEN* CLAUSES

Sentences in English often have more than one clause. A clause is a group of words that has a subject and a verb. In the examples below, each sentence has a *when* clause and a main clause.

when clause   main clause

When warm air rises,   it turns into water vapor.

when clause   main clause

When water vapor cools,   it turns into tiny drops of water or ice.

The *when* clause and the main clause can also be in reverse order. In that case, there is no comma between the two clauses.

main clause   *when* clause

Warm air turns into water vapor   **when it rises.**

main clause   *when* clause

Water vapor turns into water or ice   **when it cools.**

1 Underline seven sentences in the text "Clouds" that include a *when* clause. How many of these sentences have commas that separate the *when* clause from the main clause?

2 Complete the sentences below, using information from the text "Clouds" and the boxed text "The Latin Origin of Cloud Names." Add either a *when* clause or a main clause, as appropriate, and use commas correctly. Compare your sentences with a partner's.

1 When water vapor rises _____.

2 It is probably not going to rain _____.

3 When children draw clouds _____.

4 We call it fog _____.

5 When you see cumulonimbus clouds _____.

Task 5   WRITING AN OBSERVATION REPORT

Students in science classes often write observation reports. In these reports, they record what they see and examine that information carefully.

Write an observation report about clouds and weather. Follow the instructions below.

1 Work with a partner. Go outside, or look out the window, and look up at the sky. What is the weather like today? What kinds of clouds do you see? Describe the clouds in as much detail as you can.

2 Discuss the following question with your partner: Do your observations of the clouds and the weather agree or disagree with the information you read in the text "Clouds"? Explain why or why not.

3 Write a report about your observations. You can use the model below for help, but remember that it is just a brief example. In your own report, write as many details as you can about the clouds and the weather. Include a picture of the different types of clouds you saw.

Name: _____

Date: _____

Observation Report

Today there are _____ clouds in the sky. They are _____ clouds. According to the text "Clouds," when you see _____ clouds, the weather is usually _____. This is true / not true about the weather today. Today's weather is, in fact, _____.

Chapter 5   Writing Assignment

You are going to write a paragraph about auroras. An aurora is a natural sight in the atmosphere. Look at the photograph and read the notes below. Find a picture of an aurora in color, either in the library or on the Internet. Follow the steps and the guidelines below.

1 Discuss the information in the notes with a partner. Figure out what the symbols and abbreviations represent. Use a dictionary to look up new words, if necessary.

Auroras
- *auroras = beautiful lights in sky*
- *usually green-yellow (can be red, blue, violet)*
- *diff. shapes & sizes*
- *occur in thermosphere*
- *100–300+ km above Earth*
- *particles from sun + atmospheric gases above N. and S. poles → auroras*
- *ex. of famous auroras:*
  - *1. aurora borealis = Northern Lights*
    - *best seen from Alaska, E. Canada, Iceland (Sept.–Oct. & Mar.)*
  - *2. aurora australis = Southern Lights*
    - *best seen from Antarctica*

Aurora borealis

2 Now use the notes to write a paragraph about auroras.

> **Guidelines**
> - Include a topic sentence, at least five supporting sentences, and a concluding sentence.
> - Include any relevant information you learned in this chapter.
> - Present your ideas in a logical order.
> - Try to use *when* clauses and expressions of height where appropriate (see the Language Focus tasks, pages 107 and 113).

3 When you finish writing, exchange paragraphs with a partner and read each other's work. Then discuss the following questions about both paragraphs:

1 Did your partner include any information that you didn't include in your paragraph?

2 Does your partner's paragraph have a topic sentence and a concluding sentence?

3 Are all the supporting sentences on topic? Are there any irrelevant sentences?

4 Think about any changes to your paragraph that would improve it. Then write a second draft of the paragraph.

Preparing to read

THINKING ABOUT THE TOPIC BEFORE YOU READ

Work with a partner or a small group and do the following activities.

1| Brainstorm a list of words that describe weather, such as *hot*, *cold*, and *windy*.

2| Describe the weather today. Use some of the words you brainstormed in step 1.

3| Look at the photograph on the right and describe the weather.

4| Compare the weather in the photograph to the typical weather where you live.

5| Read the following list of places.* Guess which ones have similar weather. Divide the places into three groups, using the chart below.

Alaska (U.S.)   Puerto Rico
Gobi Desert, China   Sahara Desert, Africa
Hawaii (U.S.)   Rub' al-Khali, Saudi Arabia
Nord, Greenland   Thailand
Northern Canada

Group 1	Group 2	Group 3

6| Discuss your chart with your classmates, and explain how you divided the places into groups.

Now read

Now read the text "Climates Around the World." When you finish, turn to the tasks on page 119.

---

* You can find many of the countries referred to in this chapter on the map of the world on pages 210–211.

Weather and Climate

1 CLIMATES AROUND THE WORLD

What is the weather like today? Is it hot or cold? Is it sunny, rainy, or snowy? Weather is the atmospheric conditions at a particular time. Climate is different from weather. Climate means the average weather conditions of an area over a long period of time, at least 30 years. An area's climate includes its average temperature and its average amount of **precipitation**. Climate determines where different kinds of plants and animals can live. For example, tropical rain forests are located in hot, wet climates, and polar bears live in cold climates.

Scientists divide Earth into climate zones, or areas, according to temperature and precipitation. Some of the main climate zones are tropical, dry, mild, and polar. Tropical climates are located near the equator. They have warm temperatures all year and a lot of rain. Hawaii, Puerto Rico, and Thailand are all places with tropical climates. Dry climates have very little precipitation, so they do not have a lot of plant life. The Gobi Desert in China and the Sahara Desert in Africa are good examples of dry climates.

1

2

precipitation

any type of water in the air, for example, rain, snow, sleet, and hail

117

Mild climates have neither very hot nor very cold temperatures. It rains, but not as heavily as in tropical climates. For example, San Francisco and London are cities with mild climates. Polar climates are the coldest areas on Earth. Even during the warmest months, average temperatures are below 10 degrees Celsius (50 degrees Fahrenheit). Polar climates are also very dry, with less than 38 centimeters of precipitation each year. The Arctic (including parts of Alaska, Canada, Greenland, and other areas around the North Pole) has a polar climate.

Scientists tell us that Earth's climate is changing in important ways. For example, air and ocean temperatures have been rising in recent years. This change is called **global warming**. Scientists believe that global warming is causing other climate changes on our planet, such as an increase in heat waves and more powerful storms all over the world.

global warming

the increase over time in the temperature of Earth's atmosphere

Cherrapunji: A Place of Extremes

Does it rain very much where you live? Do you get tired of wearing a raincoat and carrying an umbrella? If so, be glad you don't live in Cherrapunji, India. Some people think Cherrapunji may be the wettest place on Earth. In fact, it is one of the rainiest places on our planet, with an average rainfall of more than 1,143 centimeters per year. However, all that rain falls during six months of the year. The rest of the year, Cherrapunji actually has a shortage of water. How is this possible?

Cherrapunji is a mountain town in the northeastern state of Meghalaya. For six months of the year, winds called monsoons blow from the southwest, and they bring extremely heavy rain. The other half of the year, the monsoons blow from the northeast, and there is almost no rain. In the past, the area around Cherrapunji was mostly forest land, and the trees protected the soil. Therefore, the ground was able to store water from the rainy season for use throughout the year. However, in recent years the town has grown, and large numbers of trees have been cut down to make room for new homes and businesses. Now that the trees are gone, most of the rainwater runs down into the valley below instead of going into the ground. That's why one of the rainiest places in the world must bring in water from other areas during the dry season.

A resident of Cherrapunji, India, gets water from a community tap.

After you read

Task 1 APPLYING WHAT YOU HAVE READ

> Applying what you have read to new subject matter helps you to see how well you understood the text.

Study the chart below. Fill in the climate for each place, based on the information in the text "Climates Around the World." Write *tropical*, *dry*, *mild*, or *polar*.

Place	Average annual temperature	Average annual precipitation	Climate
1 Manila, Philippines	27°C / 81°F	206 cm	
2 Inuvik, Canada	–9.5°C / 15°F	27 cm	
3 Namib Desert, Namibia	16°C / 61°F	5 cm	
4 Yakutsk, Russia	–10°C / 14°F	20 cm	
5 Monrovia, Liberia	26°C / 79°F	513 cm	
6 Santiago, Chile	14°C / 57°F	38 cm	

Task 2 BUILDING VOCABULARY: DEFINING KEY WORDS

> In academic texts, look for the definitions of key words in the margin as well as in the text.

Look back at the text "Climates Around the World" and find the key words listed in the left column below. Then match the words with the definitions on the right.

_____ 1 precipitation

_____ 2 equator

_____ 3 climate zone

_____ 4 Celsius

_____ 5 global warming

a a scale for measuring temperature

b an increase in the temperature of Earth's atmosphere

c rain, snow, sleet, and hail

d an imaginary line around the middle of Earth

e an area of land that has similar average temperatures and amounts of precipitation in every part

Task 3 UNDERSTANDING AVERAGES

> Scientific texts often use averages to talk about things that are measured in numbers. An average is a number that represents every thing in a group, divided by the number of the things. To calculate an average, add all the numbers for the group together. For example, the average of *2, 3,* and *10* is *5* because *2 + 3 + 10 = 15* and *15 ÷ 3 = 5.*

1 Look at the information below about Amman, Jordan. Then study the calculation of Amman's average annual (yearly) temperature.

Temperature scales*

Fahrenheit		Celsius
212		100
194		90
176		80
158		70
140		60
122		50
104		40
86		30
68		20
50		10
32		0
14		-10
-4		-20
-22		-30
-40		-40

Average Monthly Temperatures in Amman

January	8°C	July	25°C
February	9°C	August	26°C
March	12°C	September	24°C
April	16°C	October	21°C
May	21°C	November	15°C
June	24°C	December	10°C

> Average annual temperature = sum of monthly temperatures ÷ by 12 months:
>
> Monthly temperatures: 8 + 9 + 12 + 16 + 21 + 24 + 25 + 26 + 24 + 21 + 15 + 10
> Sum of monthly temperatures = 211
> Monthly temperatures, divided by 12 months = 211 ÷ 12 = 17.6
>
> The average annual temperature in Amman, Jordan is 17.6° Celsius (63.7° Fahrenheit).

2 Using the information below, calculate the average annual temperature in Buenos Aires, Argentina. Then write the answer in a sentence on a separate piece of paper.

Average Monthly Temperatures in Buenos Aires

January	23°C	July	10°C
February	22°C	August	11°C
March	20°C	September	13°C
April	16°C	October	16°C
May	13°C	November	19°C
June	10°C	December	22°C

3 Now calculate the average summer temperatures in Amman (June, July, August) and Buenos Aires (December, January, February). Write a compound sentence that states the average summer temperatures in these places. (Review "Writing Simple and Compound Sentences" on page 31, if necessary.)

---

* You can find formulas for converting one temperature scale to another on page 209.

Task 4 LANGUAGE FOCUS: INTRODUCING EXAMPLES

One way to make your writing stronger and more interesting is to include specific examples. Two common expressions for introducing examples are *for example* and *such as*.

- *For example* introduces a sentence.

  For example, rain forests grow in hot, wet climates.

- *Such as* introduces a noun or a list of nouns within a sentence.

  Rain forests have many different types of animals, **such as** gorillas, parrots, and crocodiles.

Notice that there is a comma after *for example* and a comma before *such as*.

1 Look back at the text "Climates Around the World" and underline all the examples that are introduced with *for example* and *such as*.

2 Read the following text about global warming.

> Our planet is getting warmer, and people are concerned about it. Although some temperature change is natural, temperatures on Earth have increased much faster than expected in recent years.
>
> Global warming is causing some troubling climate changes. Unfortunately, people around the world are adding to the problem by using more and more energy for heat, electricity, and transportation. Most of this energy is produced by burning fossil fuels. This increases global warming. To slow global warming and help prevent further damage to the planet, people need to make some changes in their daily lives.

3 Now read the sentences and phrases below. Each one is an example that explains an idea in the text more fully. Decide where you could add each of these examples. Then rewrite the text on a separate piece of paper, including the additional examples.

   a For example, they could recycle more things, walk more, and drive less.
   b For example, some areas are having more heat waves, others are getting heavier rain, and polar areas are getting warmer.
   c such as oil, gas, and coal
   d For example, over the 100 years of the twentieth century, temperatures increased by 0.5°C. However, before that time, it took 400 years for temperatures to increase by the same amount.

Preparing to read

PREVIEWING KEY PARTS OF A TEXT

1 | Preview the title, the headings, and the photographs of the text on pages 123–124 to get a general idea of what it is about. Read the first sentence of each paragraph. Then answer the questions below.

    1 What is the text about?

    2 What two types of storms does the text discuss? Write the names of the storms next to the pictures below.

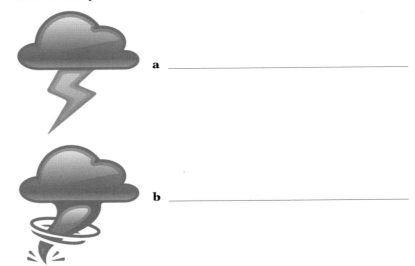

a _____

b _____

2 | Based on your preview of the text, write *T* (true) or *F* (false) next to each of the following sentences.

    _____ **1** There are only a few thunderstorms every year.

    _____ **2** Most thunderstorms do not last a long time.

    _____ **3** Thunderstorms can cause tornadoes.

    _____ **4** Tornadoes are most common in Europe.

    _____ **5** Scientists know everything about thunderstorms and tornadoes.

Now read

Now read the text "Storms." When you finish, turn to the tasks on page 125.

2 STORMS

Thunderstorms

At this moment, almost 2,000 thunderstorms are occurring around the world. Thunderstorms are different from rain showers because they produce thunder and **lightning**. Lightning is electricity that moves between clouds, or between a cloud and the ground. Lightning heats the air around it. The hot air expands and then quickly contracts as it cools down. This movement of air makes the sound called thunder. Thunder and lightning happen at almost the exact same time. However, because light moves faster than sound, people see lightning before they hear thunder.

1

lightning
a flash of bright light in the sky, caused by electricity during a thunderstorm

Approximately 90 percent of thunderstorms are small and last no longer than 30 minutes. These short thunderstorms bring cool rain on a hot, humid day. However, 10 percent are powerful storms that can produce hail, strong winds, heavy rain, and tornadoes. Severe thunderstorms can continue for hours and even days, and they can cause a lot of damage. Every year, lightning causes over 7,000 forest fires, hundreds of injuries, and more than 90 deaths in the United States. Hail is another destructive and costly problem. It causes almost $1 billion of damage each year. However, the most dangerous part of severe thunderstorms is heavy rain, because it can cause flooding. More deaths result from flooding than from lightning or hail.

2

Tornadoes

Severe thunderstorms can also cause tornadoes. Tornadoes, or "twisters," are tall, spinning funnel-shaped clouds that touch the ground. They are usually over in 15 minutes or less, but they move quickly and cause a great deal of damage in just a few minutes. The air inside a tornado spins very fast, more than 480 kilometers per hour, as it moves quickly upward. Tornadoes can lift trees, cars, people, animals, and even houses into the air.

3

Tornadoes occur throughout the world, but they are most common in the United States, where more than 1,000 tornadoes occur each year. Most of them occur in "Tornado Alley," an area in the central

4

part of the country. Within this area, the states of Texas and Oklahoma experience the most tornadoes. On average, more than 100 tornadoes strike Texas each year. That is approximately the same number of tornadoes that strike the whole country of Canada in one year.

Today, scientists still have many questions about severe thunderstorms and tornadoes. They continue to do research in order to better understand, predict, and prepare people for these destructive storms.

5

Hail

Hail consists of balls of ice called hailstones. Hailstones form inside storm clouds when cold water freezes around pieces of dust. The stones can be as small as a pea or as large as a grapefruit. The largest hailstone ever measured in the United States fell in Aurora, Nevada, on June 22, 2003. It had a diameter of approximately 18 centimeters and a circumference (distance around the outside) of almost 48 centimeters.

Hail can be very dangerous and destructive. For example, on May 5, 1995, approximately 10,000 people were enjoying an outdoor festival in Fort Worth, Texas. Suddenly, a powerful thunderstorm started. Hailstones as large as baseballs fell from the sky at 128 kilometers per hour. They hit people as they ran for safety, and they broke car windows. Strong winds damaged buildings, heavy rain caused flooding, and thousands of homes lost power. The storm killed 13 people, injured more than 100, and caused $2 billion of damage.

After you read

Task 1 USING A VENN DIAGRAM TO ORGANIZE IDEAS FROM A TEXT

Academic texts often discuss two or more related topics. Although these topics may share some information, each one has its own supporting details. You can use a Venn diagram to organize information from related texts.

Venn diagrams use overlapping circles to show relationships. They can show information that is true only for topic "A," other information that is true only for topic "B," and information that is true for both topics ("A + B"). The shared information is shown in the overlapping areas of the circles.

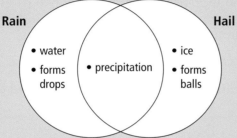

1 Below is a list of details from the text "Storms." Write *TH* next to the details about thunderstorms, *TO* next to the details about tornadoes, and *B* next to the details that describe both storms.

_____ are fast moving   _____ can lift houses into the air

_____ can cause a lot of damage   _____ can produce lightning and hail

_____ are tall, spinning clouds   _____ happen throughout the world

_____ happen more than 1,000 times a day _____ can cause dangerous flooding

2 Copy the Venn diagram below on a separate piece of paper. Then complete the diagram. Write the details from step 1 in the correct places.

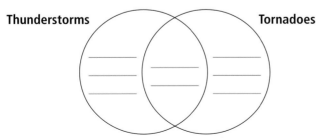

3 Add at least one more detail from the text to each circle of the Venn diagram. Then add another detail to the overlapping area.

Task 2 BUILDING VOCABULARY: USING A DICTIONARY

Sometimes you will need a dictionary to help you figure out the meaning of a word in a text. Many words have more than one definition. It is important to choose the definition that is appropriate for the context in which you see the word.

The sentences below are from the text "Storms." In each sentence, the word in **bold** has more than one meaning. Use your dictionary and the context of the sentence to choose the correct part of speech and definition for each word.

Example:

The hot air expands and then quickly **contracts** as it cools down.

contract (*n.*) 1. a written legal agreement between two people or companies that says what each will do. 2. an agreement to kill someone for money. (*v.*) 1. to get an illness. 2. to become smaller.

Correct definition: <u>(v.) to become smaller</u>

1 These **short** thunderstorms bring cool rain on a hot, humid day.

Correct definition: _____

2 Approximately 90 percent of thunderstorms are small, and they don't **last** longer than 30 minutes.

Correct definition: _____

3 Every year, lightning causes **over** 7,000 forest fires, hundreds of injuries, and more than 90 deaths in the United States.

Correct definition: _____

4 They are usually **over** in 15 minutes or less, but they move quickly and cause a lot of damage in just a few minutes.

Correct definition: _____

5 On average, more than 100 tornadoes **strike** Texas each year.

Correct definition: _____

Task 3 LANGUAGE FOCUS: USING *THIS* / *THAT* / *THESE* / *THOSE* TO CONNECT IDEAS

Writers often use *this*, *that*, *these*, and *those*, followed by a noun or noun phrase, to help connect the ideas in different sentences.

noun phrase

Hail sometimes falls during a severe thunderstorm. **These** balls of ice can hurt people and damage crops.

The phrase *these balls of ice* refers back to *hail* in the preceding sentence, and helps the reader understand that hail means "balls of ice."

Reread paragraphs 1, 2, 4, and 5 of the text and find examples of phrases with *this*, *that*, *these*, or *those*. Write each phrase and the idea it refers back to.

1 Paragraph 1

Phrase: *This movement of air*

Refers back to: *The hot air expands and then quickly contracts . . . .*

2 Paragraph 2

Phrase:

Refers back to:

3 Paragraph 4

Phrase:

Refers back to:

4 Paragraph 5

Phrase:

Refers back to:

Task 4 EXAMINING STATISTICS

It is not always possible to provide a statistic as an exact number. There-fore, writers often use words and phrases, such as *almost*, *approximately*, *over*, and *more than*, before a statistic to make it less exact.

Hail causes **almost** $1 billion of damage each year.

The word *almost* makes the statistic ($1 billion) less exact. The sentence means that hail causes less than $1 billion of damage each year, but very close to $1 billion.

1 Look back at the text "Storms." Underline the statistics and circle the word or phrase that makes each statistic less exact.

2 Based on the statistics and words you found in step 1, answer the following questions:

1 How many thunderstorms might be happening at this moment?
  a 1,000
  b 1,987
  c 2,238

2 Last week there was a tornado in Texas. How many minutes did it probably last?
  a 10
  b 25
  c 50

3 How many tornadoes will probably occur in the United States next year?
  a 100
  b 1,000
  c 1,100

4 Firefighters think that lighting will cause _____ forest fires next year.
  a 6,800
  b 7,200
  c 7,000

5 How many tornadoes will probably strike Canada next year?
  a 110
  b 50
  c 1,000

Task 5 INCLUDING STATISTICS IN YOUR WRITING

Using statistics in your writing is one way to support your ideas. Remember that you don't always have to give exact numbers. It is usually easier for a reader to understand a text if the statistics are approximate (rounded up or down to the nearest whole number). For example, you can round 46.7 centimeters up to 47 centimeters, and you can round 46.3 centimeters down to 46 centimeters.

1 Read the following information about one type of powerful storm.

> Nor'easters are powerful storms that occur along the east coast of the United States. They are named for the winds that blow from the northeast. Nor'easters produce heavy snow, rain, wind, and giant waves that often cause serious flooding and damage. Such powerful snowstorms are sometimes called blizzards. In 1978, an especially powerful nor'easter hit the state of Massachusetts. People called it the Blizzard of 1978.

2 Write a paragraph about the 1978 nor'easter on a separate piece of paper. Follow these steps:

1 Copy and complete the topic sentence below to start your paragraph.

The Blizzard of 1978 _____

2 Write four to six supporting sentences based on the statistics below. Use numbers, words, and phrases (*almost*, *approximately*, *over*, *more than*) to make the statistics less exact.

Statistics for the Blizzard of 1978

- caused $502 million of damage
- lasted 32 hours and 40 minutes
- damaged 9,406 houses
- destroyed 2,163 houses
- killed 73 people in Massachusetts
- dumped 66 centimeters of snow on the city of Boston, Massachusetts
- forced 17,008 people to go to emergency shelters

Boston, Massachusetts, winter 1978

3 End your paragraph with a concluding sentence.

Preparing to read

THINKING ABOUT THE TOPIC BEFORE YOU READ

Discuss the following question with your classmates:

Did you ever experience a hurricane? If so, describe where you were and what happened.

INCREASING YOUR READING SPEED

1 Review the strategies for increasing your reading speed on page 66.

2 Write your starting time. Then read the text "Hurricanes," using the speed-reading strategies. For this task, do not read the boxed text, "The Benefits of Wind," on page 132.

Starting time: _____

3 Fill in the time you finished.

Finishing time: _____

Then calculate your reading speed:
Number of words in the text (493) ÷
Number of minutes it took you to
read the text = your reading speed

Reading speed: _____

Your goal should be about 80–100 words per minute.

4 Check your reading comprehension. Circle the correct answers without looking at the text.

1 Hurricanes form over (warm waters / cold waters / land).

2 Hurricanes have (one / two / three) main parts.

3 Hurricanes can cause a lot of (noise / damage / happiness).

4 Hurricanes can be (deadly / costly / deadly and costly).

5 Many scientists think there will be (more / fewer / no) hurricanes in the future.

Now read

Now read the text "Hurricanes" again, including the boxed text. Then check your answers to step 4 above. When you finish, turn to the tasks on page 133.

3 HURRICANES

People in China call them typhoons. People in India refer to them as tropical cyclones. People in the United States call them hurricanes. Although people use different names, they are referring to the same thing: a very powerful, spinning storm that causes strong winds, heavy rain, and giant waves.

The formation of a hurricane

A hurricane begins near the equator, over warm tropical waters. It might start in the southern part of the North Atlantic Ocean, the Caribbean Sea, the Gulf of Mexico, or the East Pacific Ocean. The storm starts as an area of thunderstorms. It continues to grow, and the winds blow furiously in a circular path. When the winds reach 118 kilometers per hour, the storm is called a hurricane. The source of a hurricane's energy is the warm ocean water it travels over. As it moves over colder waters or over land, it weakens.

The parts of a hurricane

Hurricanes have three main parts: the eye, the eyewall, and the spiral rain bands. The eye of a hurricane is a calm area with only light winds, right in the middle of the spinning storm. The eyewall is a wall of clouds around the eye. The eyewall contains the strongest winds and the most rain. Rain bands are long strips of thunderclouds that also follow a circular path around the eye of the hurricane, but they are farther away than the eyewall. Like the eyewall, rain bands bring rain and strong winds.

spiral rain bands

eye

eyewall

Hurricane damage

The hurricane's strong winds move it across the ocean. If a hurricane reaches land, the powerful winds, heavy rain, and **storm surge** can cause death and destruction. Hurricane winds can blow more than 320 kilometers per hour. They can knock down trees, destroy buildings, and blow heavy objects through the air. Although the strong winds cause great harm, water usually produces the most damage. More than 60 centimeters of rain can fall in one day, and the storm surge can be as high as 6 meters. All this water can wash away beaches, roads, bridges, homes, crops, animals, and people.

storm surge

a sudden rise in the ocean's water level as it moves closer to land during a storm

Hurricane damage can be overwhelming. In 2005, Hurricane Katrina caused more than $80 billion of damage. It killed more than 1,500 people and destroyed more than 250,000 homes in the southeastern part of the United States. Although Katrina was the costliest hurricane in United States history, the Galveston, Texas, hurricane in 1900 was the deadliest. More than 8,000 people died in that storm. However, the deadliest hurricane of all was the 1970 Bangladesh cyclone. It killed more than 300,000 people and devastated the country.

Hurricanes and global warming

Hurricanes are the most destructive storms on earth, and no one knows how to stop them. Many scientists believe that as global warming continues, and ocean temperatures keep rising, there will be more and more hurricanes in the future. Throughout the world, people are working to improve hurricane forecasting and emergency planning so that we can be better prepared for these devastating storms. At the same time, people are looking for ways to slow down global warming and to reduce its extremely destructive effects.

wind turbine
a tall, thin, metal windmill that produces electricity

The Benefits of Wind

Hurricane and tornado winds can be destructive and deadly. However, wind can also be a positive force. In fact, some people are using the power of wind to produce energy. For example, Germany, Spain, and the United States use **wind turbines** to generate electricity in some areas, and they are becoming more popular in other countries, too.

Wind energy has many advantages. It is a cheap way to produce electricity, it is a clean source of power, and it is unlimited. As long as the wind blows, people can use it to produce energy. However, wind energy has a few disadvantages. For example, wind turbines are useful only in areas with strong, regular winds so they cannot be used everywhere. In addition, some people think they are ugly.

Although there are problems with wind power, it is a clean, low-cost, and renewable way to produce energy. It may also help us solve two of our planet's most serious problems: pollution and global warming.

A field of wind turbines near Palm Springs, California

After you read

Task 1 READING FOR MAIN IDEAS

1 Look back at the text "Hurricanes" and write the number of the paragraph that deals with each of the following topics:

   1 the three parts of a hurricane   par. _____
   2 the connection between global warming and hurricanes   par. _____
   3 different names for hurricanes   par. _____
   4 the power of a hurricane   par. _____
   5 the damage that specific hurricanes have caused   par. _____
   6 how hurricanes form   par. _____

2 Check (✔) the sentence that expresses the main idea of the whole text.

   _____ **a** Scientists believe that global warming may cause more hurricanes in
          the future.

   _____ **b** Hurricanes are deadly storms.

   _____ **c** Hurricanes are powerful storms that can cause a lot of damage
          and destruction.

3 Compare your answers with a partner's.

Task 2 BUILDING VOCABULARY: SYNONYMS

Synonyms are words that have similar meanings (for example, *big* and
large). You can use synonyms to avoid using the same words again and
again. This will make your writing more interesting.

1 Find and underline the following words in the text "Hurricanes."

   1 call (*v.*) _____ (par. 1)   **4** destruction (*n.*) _____ (par. 4)
   2 begins (*v.*) _____ (par. 2)   **5** destructive (*adj.*) _____ (par 6)
   3 strong (*adj.*) _____ (par. 4)

2 Find and circle a synonym for each word in step 1. You will find the word and its
synonym in the same paragraph. Write each synonym next to the appropriate word
in step 1.

3 Choose one pair of synonyms and use them to write two connected sentences of
your own.

   *Last year, there was a devastating tornado in my city. The destructive storm caused
   hundreds of injuries.*

Task 3 LANGUAGE FOCUS: PREPOSITIONS OF LOCATION

Prepositions of location show the spatial relationship between two or more things. For example, in the diagram below:

- The circle is **over** the square.
- The square is **near** the heart.
- The triangle is **in** the heart.
- The heart is **around** the triangle.

1 | In the sentences below, circle the preposition that shows location and underline the two things it relates. Then draw a simple diagram showing the physical relationship between these two things.

   1 Hurricanes form near the equator.

   2 Some hurricanes form over the warm waters of the Gulf of Mexico.

   3 The eye of a hurricane is in the middle of the spinning storm.

   4 Rain bands circle around the eye of the hurricane.

2 Look at the photograph below. Work with a partner, and take turns describing what you see. Use prepositions that show location.

Examples:
> *The boat is in the street.*
> *The helicopter is over the houses.*

Task 4   THINKING CRITICALLY ABOUT THE TOPIC

In class and on tests, you will often have to think about the ideas in a text in relation to your own knowledge and experience.

Discuss the following questions in a small group.

1 What have you noticed or heard about Earth's changing climate?

2 What are some things you can do to help slow global warming?

3 Some people, companies, and countries have made changes to help slow global warming, and others have not. Why do you think this is true?

Chapter 6   Writing Assignment

Write a paragraph about the climate in a place you know. You can write about the place where you live now or some place where you have lived or visited in the past. Describe the climate in as much detail as you can. Discuss the weather conditions that are common in the area. Find some additional information in the library or on the Internet. Follow the steps and the guidelines below.

1 Decide on the place you are going to write about, and make some notes about two or three important ideas that you want to include in your paragraph.

2 Discuss your ideas with a partner or in a small group.

3 Then, on your own, think of at least one detail or example to support each idea.

4 Now write the first draft of your paragraph.

Guidelines

- Include a topic sentence, at least one supporting sentence for each idea, and a concluding sentence.
- Include any relevant information you learned in this chapter. Remember to present your ideas in a logical order.
- Use examples and statistics to explain and support your ideas. Introduce examples with *for example* and *such as* where appropriate (see the Language Focus task, page 121).
- Use prepositions of location correctly. (see the Language Focus task, page 134).
- Give the paragraph a title.

---

5 When you finish writing, exchange paragraphs with a partner and read each other's work. Then discuss the following questions about both paragraphs:

   1 What is the most interesting information in your partner's paragraph?

   2 Does your partner's paragraph have correct form and structure?

   3 Are all the ideas presented in a logical order?

   4 Is there a detail or example that supports each idea?

6 Think about any changes to your paragraph that would improve it. Then write a second draft of the paragraph.

Life on Earth

In this unit, we look at living things in the natural world. In Chapter 7, we discuss the features that all living things share. We also examine plant and animal life. In the last two chapters, we explore humans. In Chapter 8, we focus on parts of the human body: the brain, the skeletal and muscular systems, and the heart and circulatory system. Finally, in Chapter 9, we look at why humans are living longer today. We then take a look at the effects our growing population has on the natural world.

Previewing the unit

Read the contents page for Unit 4, and do the following activities.

Chapter 7: Plants and Animals

This chapter describes life on earth, focusing on plants and animals.

1 | Go outside, or look out the window. Make a list of all the living things you see. Then make a list of all the things you see that are not alive, such as rocks. Compare your lists with a partner. What do you think all living things have in common?

2 | Read the list of features below. Label each feature either *P* (plants) or *A* (animals). Then add one more feature of plants and one more feature of animals.

_____ 1 have leaves

_____ 2 have a brain

_____ 3 raise their young

_____ 4 can make their own food

_____ 5 can communicate with each other

_____ 6 produce oxygen

Chapter 8: The Human Body

This chapter focuses on various parts of the human body. How much do you know about the body? Mark *T* (true) or *F* (false) next to each of the following sentences:

_____ 1 The heart is a muscle.

_____ 2 The brain is a bone.

_____ 3 The brain is bigger than the heart.

_____ 4 Bones are heavy.

_____ 5 There are 105 muscles in the body.

_____ 6 The rib bones protect the heart.

Chapter 9: Living Longer, Living Better?

This chapter examines why humans are living longer these days, and what that means for the natural world.

1 | Why do you think people are living longer these days? Do you think human lives are better or worse today than they were in the past? Explain your answer.

2 | Do you think humans have a good effect or a bad effect on plants, animals, and other parts of the natural world? Give examples to support your ideas.

Unit Contents 4

Preparing to read

THINKING ABOUT THE TOPIC BEFORE YOU READ

1 Read the sentences below and check (✔) the ones you think are true.

_____ **1** All living things need water.

_____ **2** All living things need a place to live.

_____ **3** All living things need air to breathe.

_____ **4** All living things need food.

_____ **5** All living things grow.

_____ **6** All living things die someday.

2 Compare your answers with a partner's.

3 With your partner, add two more true sentences to the list. Share your ideas with the class.

BUILDING BACKGROUND KNOWLEDGE ABOUT THE TOPIC

Read the following information about cells.

> All living things are made up of cells. A cell is the smallest unit of life. All cells have an outer covering called a cell membrane. Inside every cell is a jelly-like material called cytoplasm. Most cells also have a nucleus in the middle of the cytoplasm.

Look at the diagram of a cell below and label the three main parts: *cell membrane*, *cytoplasm*, and *nucleus*.

Now read

Now read the text "Living Things." When you finish, turn to the tasks on page 143.

Plants and Animals

1 LIVING THINGS

What is the difference between a rock on the ground and a plant that grows next to it? What is the difference between the ocean and a fish that lives there? What is the difference between a cloud in the sky and a bird that flies through it? What do plants, fish, and birds have in common? They are all **organisms**, or living things, but rocks, the ocean, and clouds are not.

organism
| a living thing

Life on Earth is extremely diverse, or full of differences. If you look around, you will notice that organisms are many different shapes and sizes. Some, like ants, are very small. Others, like whales, are quite large. Organisms also live in a variety of places. Some live in the air, others live in or on the earth, and many live in the ocean. Although organisms are different from each other in these ways, they are similar in other ways. For example, they all need food for energy, water, and a place to live. In addition, all organisms grow, develop, and eventually die.

Another important similarity is that all organisms are composed of cells. A **cell** is the smallest unit of life. Most cells are so small that you can only see them with a **microscope**. All cells have an outer covering, called a cell membrane. This membrane keeps the cell material inside the cell. It also controls the movement of things into and out of the cell. For example, the membrane allows water to move into and out of a cell, but it does not allow dangerous materials to enter. Inside every cell is a jelly-like material called cytoplasm. Most cells also have a nucleus in the middle of the cytoplasm. The nucleus controls all activity in the cell. 3

Most organisms on Earth are made up of just one cell. For example, both bacteria and algae are single-celled organisms. Other larger organisms, such as many plants and all humans, are multicellular organisms. They are made up of many cells. In fact, the human body is made up of billions of cells. 4

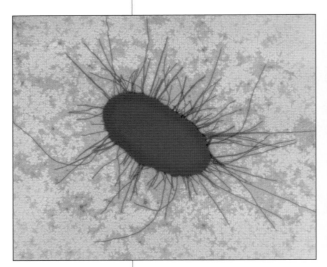

A bacteria cell

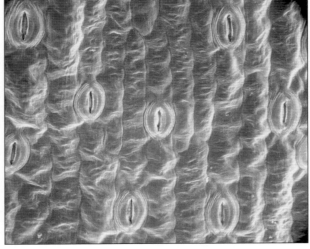

Leaf cells

The cells in multicellular organisms work together. A group of cells that work together to do one job is called a tissue. For example, one group of thousands of cells forms muscle tissue in the body. When two or more different types of tissues work together, they form an organ, such as a person's heart, an elephant's ear, or a plant's leaf. When a group of organs works together, they form an organ system, such as the circulatory system (the system that transports food and gases through the body with the help of the heart and lungs). 5

Biologists (scientists who study living things) continue to learn more and more about the organisms on our planet. Some of their research findings may help us protect the rich diversity of life on Earth in the future. 6

After you read

Task 1 TEST TAKING: ANSWERING TRUE/FALSE QUESTIONS

1 Review the strategies for answering true/false questions on page 35. Next, write *T* (true) or *F* (false) in the blank before each of the sentences below. Then write the number of the paragraph where you found the information in the text "Living Things."

_____ **1** Some organisms need water.   par. _____

_____ **2** Organisms grow and die.   par. _____

_____ **3** Humans, animals, and plants have organs.   par. _____

_____ **4** Bacteria and humans are multicellular organisms.   par. _____

_____ **5** All cells have cell membranes, cytoplasm, and a nucleus.   par. _____

_____ **6** Rocks, fish, and birds are all organisms.   par. _____

_____ **7** You often need a microscope to see a cell.   par. _____

_____ **8** Some organisms are made up of many cells.   par. _____

2 Work with a partner. Correct the sentences you marked false in step 1.

Task 2 BUILDING VOCABULARY: WORD FAMILIES

When you learn a new word, try to learn some other words in its word family as well. This will develop your vocabulary. For example, when you learn the verb *destroy* you can also learn the related words *destruction* (*n*.) and *destructive* (*adj*.).

1 Find a word in the text "Living Things" that is related to each of the words below. Write the part of speech next to each word. Use the abbreviations *n*., *v*., and *adj*.

1 life *(n.) living (adj.)*   **4** cell _____ _____

2 difference _____ _____   **5** movement _____ _____

3 similarity _____ _____   **6** diversity _____ _____

2 Complete each sentence below with an appropriate word from step 1.

1 Fish and birds live in _____ places.

2 Bacteria are made up of just one _____.

3 Many materials _____ into and out of a cell.

4 Plant cells are _____ to animal cells. They have many things in common.

5 There is a lot of _____ on Earth. There are many different kinds of organisms.

Task 3 · ASKING FOR CLARIFICATION

When you are not sure about the meaning of an idea or a word in a text, you can ask questions to clarify the meaning (make it clearer).
Here are some structures you can use to ask for clarification:

- **I'm not sure what the author means when she says that . . .**
- **Could you explain what the word** _____ **means?**
- **Could you give me an example of** _____ **?**
- **I don't understand what the text means in paragraph** _____ **where it says . . .**

1 | Read the following clarification questions about the text "Living Things."

   1 I'm not sure what the author means in paragraph 3 when she says that a cell is the smallest unit of life.

   2 Could you explain what the word _circulatory_ in paragraph 5 means?

   3 Could you give me an example of another organ system in addition to the circulatory system?

   4 I don't understand what the text means in paragraph 2 where it says that all organisms develop.

2 | With a partner, answer the clarification questions in step 1.

3 | Find other words and ideas in the text that you would like to clarify. With your partner, take turns asking and answering clarification questions.

Task 4 · WRITING ABOUT SIMILARITIES

In academic texts, writers often use certain expressions to compare two or more people, places, things, or ideas. These expressions show how things are similar (alike in some ways). Look at the examples below.

Some ways to compare two things:

- Humpback whales and bottlenose dolphins **are similar (to each other)** in many ways.
- They **have** many features **in common**.
- **Both** humpback whales and bottlenose dolphins live in the ocean.
- **One similarity is that** they **are both** mammals.
- **Another similarity is that** they **both** eat fish.

Some ways to compare more than two things:

- Whales, walruses, and seals **are similar** (to each other) in many ways.
- They **have** many features **in common**.
- **One similarity is that** they **are all** mammals.
- **All** mammals have body temperatures that stay about the same.

1 Look back at the text "Living Things," and underline the expressions of similarity.

2 Complete the expressions of similarity in the sentences below. Use the structures in the box on page 144 as a guide.

   1 Roses, tulips, and orchids are _____ in many ways. One _____ is that they are _____ popular flowers.

   2 Dogs and wolves are _____ natural hunters.

   3 _____ tissues and organs are made of cells.

   4 _____ living things need food to eat and a place to live.

3 Write three sentences of your own. In each sentence, compare two animals, expressing one similarity between them. Compare your sentences with a partner's.

   1 _____

   2 _____

   3 _____

4 Read the following paragraph and discuss the questions below.

> Lions and tigers are similar in three ways. One similarity is that both animals have similar diets. Lions and tigers are both meat eaters who hunt other large and medium-size animals. Another similarity is that both animals are part of the cat family. Lions are also similar to tigers in size. Both animals are about the same weight and height. As you can see, lions and tigers have several things in common.

   1 What two things is the writer comparing?

   2 How many points of comparison does the writer discuss? What are they?

   3 Underline all the expressions of similarity in the paragraph.

5 Now write a paragraph about the similarities between dogs and cats. Remember to start with a topic sentence. Include two or three points that the animals have in common. Use some expressions of similarity, as appropriate. End with a concluding sentence.

6 Compare your paragraph with a partner's.

Preparing to read

CONDUCTING A SURVEY

The text you are going to read is about plants. Plants are an important part of life on our planet, and they provide us with many of the products we use every day.

1 | Survey five people to get more information about plants. First, copy the chart below on a separate piece of paper. Then ask each person the questions in the chart. Record their names and answers.

Name	Why are plants important?	What are three products we get from plants?
1		
2		
3		
4		
5		

2 | Share your survey results with the class.

PREVIEWING KEY PARTS OF A TEXT

Preview the title, headings, and photographs on pages 147–148 to get a general idea of what the text is about. Read the first sentence of each paragraph. Then write *T* (true) or *F* (false) next to each sentence below.

_____ **1** There are thousands of different types of plants on Earth.

_____ **2** There are three general categories of plants.

_____ **3** Earth has more seed plants than seedless plants.

_____ **4** We could survive on Earth without plants.

_____ **5** A sunflower has a flower and a stem, but no leaves.

_____ **6** Plant life on Earth is decreasing.

Now read

Now read the text "Plant Life." When you finish, turn to the tasks on page 149.

2 PLANT LIFE

The diversity of plants

There are approximately 300,000 different types of plants on Earth, and they grow almost everywhere. For example, moss and lichen grow in cold polar climates, palm trees and orchids grow in hot, wet, tropical climates, and cacti and ocotillos grow in warm, dry climates. Plants are similar to other organisms in several ways, but they also have their own special features.

1

Plant size and structure

Just like other organisms, plants come in many different sizes. For example, there are tiny ferns, which you can see only with a microscope. In contrast, consider the giant redwood trees of northern California, which can grow to more than 100 meters. Plants also have some structural features in common with other organisms. For example, plants are made up of cells, which have cell membranes, cytoplasm, and a nucleus. One difference is that plant cells also have thick, rigid cell walls that surround the membrane. These cell walls give the plant structure and support and allow it to grow straight and tall. Cell walls also help protect the cells.

2

Seedless plants and seed plants

Scientists divide plants into two categories: seedless plants and seed plants. Seedless plants grow from **spores**, not seeds. Spores are tiny cells that grow into new plants. Seedless plants do not have flowers, and most grow in places that are damp (a little wet). Mosses and ferns are examples of seedless plants.

3

spore

a cell produced by seedless plants and some other organisms that is able to grow into a new plant or organism

Ferns

Seed plants are much more common than seedless plants. All seed plants have roots, a stem, and leaves. Unlike seedless plants, many also have flowers, which produce the seeds. These seeds grow into new plants. The roots take in water from the soil. The water then travels through the stem to the leaves. The leaves take in sunlight and carbon dioxide from the air. In this way, plants get the materials they need to make their own food. Roses and sunflowers are examples of seed plants.

4

Fern spores

Sunflowers

Plants as providers

Plants give us many of the things we need to live. They provide food, clothing, paper, and wood. Some plants even function as natural medicines. However, the most important thing plants provide is oxygen, which all organisms need for survival.

5

Plants add oxygen to the air through their food-making process, called **photosynthesis**. Photosynthesis takes place in the leaves of plants, and it works in this way: Plants take in sunlight, carbon dioxide, and water to make their food, called glucose. Glucose is a kind of sugar. This process also creates oxygen, but plants do not need as much oxygen as they produce. Therefore, they release the oxygen into the air. When plants take carbon dioxide out of the air and put oxygen into it, they create air we can breathe. In fact, one acre of trees in a forest releases enough oxygen in a year to keep 18 people alive.

6

photosynthesis

the process by which a plant uses energy from the sun to make its own food

Plant loss

Although plants are essential for all of life on Earth, more plants die each year. Natural disasters, such as fires, and human activities have destroyed approximately 50 percent of the world's forests. Today, there is a growing demand for more building materials and more land to raise animals and grow crops. As a result, many trees are cut down. The effects of this deforestation, or destruction of the trees, are troubling. First of all, large numbers of plants and animals are losing their habitats. In addition, scientists believe that deforestation can cause drought (a long period of time without rain). Moreover, when there are fewer trees, there is less oxygen in the air for us to breathe. There is also more carbon dioxide, which contributes to global warming. For all these reasons, we should be very concerned as more of our green earth turns brown every day.

7

Aloe Vera: A Natural Healer

People have used aloe vera as a healing plant for more than 4,000 years. Some people call it a miracle plant because of the way it can heal injuries to the skin, such as cuts, insect bites, and burns. The leaves contain a cool, clear gel. If you burn yourself while cooking, slice open an aloe vera leaf and put the gel on the burn. The pain will probably go away in a few minutes. Many people also think aloe vera helps keep skin young and healthy. The gel is an ingredient in many brands of makeup, soap, shampoo, sunscreen, lotion, and other skin products. Because aloe vera is so popular, you will find a pot of it growing in many kitchens around the world.

Aloe vera

After you read

Task 1 NOTE TAKING: OUTLINING

> An outline is a clear way to organize notes so that they are easy to read and review. In an outline, numbers and letters show the relationships between the different parts of the text.

1 | Complete the outline below, based on the information in the text "Plant Life." In this outline, notice that Roman numerals (*I, II, III*, etc.) introduce the main ideas, and capital letters (*A, B, C*, etc.) represent the main details.

   I.   *Diversity of plants*

      A. ≈ *300,000 types of plants on Earth*

      B. *grow in lots of different _____*

   II. *Plant size and structure*

      A. *different sizes*

      B. *plant structure: made up of _____, which have cell _____, _____, a _____, and cell _____*

   III. *Seedless plants*

      A. *grow from _____, not seeds*

      B. *do not have flowers and most grow in _____ places*

   IV. *_____*

      A. *more common than seedless plants*

      B. *they have _____, _____, and _____, and they can have _____*

   V. *Products from plants*

      A. *provide us with food, clothing, paper, wood, and medicine*

      B. *most importantly, they provide _____*

   VI. *_____*

      A. *takes place in plant leaves*

      B. *the process: plants take in _____, _____, and _____, and they make _____*

      C. *process puts _____ into the air and takes out _____*

   VII. *Plant loss*

      A. *causes: _____*

      B. *effects: _____*

Task 2 BUILDING VOCABULARY: DEFINING KEY WORDS

1 Match the words in the left column below with the definitions on the right.

    _____ **1** stem

    _____ **2** oxygen

    _____ **3** roots

    _____ **4** carbon dioxide

    _____ **5** leaves

    _____ **6** flower

    a the part of a plant that gets water from the soil

    b the part of a plant that is related to making seeds

    c the gas that a plant releases into the air

    d the part of a plant that carries water from the roots to the leaves

    e the gas that a plant takes from the air

    f the part of a plant that makes food from water, the sun's rays, and carbon dioxide

2 Label the plant diagram below with the appropriate key words from step 1.

3 Add the following words to the diagram below: *sunlight*, *water*, *carbon dioxide*, and *oxygen*. What process does the diagram show? Write the name of the process under the diagram.

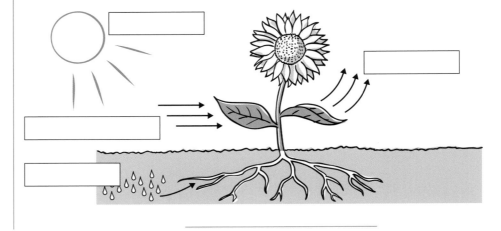

4 Look back at the text "Plant Life" to check your work.

Task 3   BUILDING VOCABULARY: CLUES THAT SIGNAL DEFINITIONS

Remember that the definition of a new word is often right there in the text. If you learn to recognize different kinds of clues, you will find the definitions. You have already learned some of these clues:

_____ (definition)

_____ , *that is,* _____

_____ , *or* _____

Here are some examples of other clues:

- A root **is** a plant part that takes in water from the soil.
- Healing plants **are** plants that people use to treat medical conditions.
- Every cell has a jelly-like material inside, **called** cytoplasm.

Look at the words in the chart below. Find these words and their definitions in the text "Plant Life." Then fill in the chart. Write the definition of each word and the clue that helped you find it.

Word	Definition	Clue
1 spores (par. 3)		
2 photosynthesis (par. 6)		
3 glucose (par. 6)		
4 deforestation (par. 7)		
5 drought (par. 7)		

Task 4 WRITING ABOUT DIFFERENCES

In academic texts, writers often use certain expressions to contrast two or more people, places, things, or ideas. These expressions show how things are different from each other. Look at these examples:

- Sunflowers grow in dry places. **In contrast**, ferns grow in places that are damp.
- **One difference between** sunflowers and ferns **is that** sunflowers grow from seeds, **but** ferns grow from spores.
- **Unlike** ferns, sunflowers have flowers.
- Sunflowers and ferns **are different** types of plants.

1 Look back at the text "Plant Life," and underline all the expressions of difference. Compare your answers with a partner's.

2 Complete the expressions of difference in the sentences below. Use the structures in the box above as a guide.

1 Moss and palm trees are very _____ types of plants.

2 Moss grows in cold climates. _____ _____, palm trees grow in tropical climates.

3 One _____ between moss and palm trees is their height. Palm trees are tall, but moss is short.

4 Palm trees can make their own food, _____ moss cannot.

5 _____ moss, palm trees grow from seeds.

3 Choose two plants that are different from each other. Write three or four sentences that contrast the plants. Use the structures in the box above as a guide. Compare your sentences with a partner's.

1 _____

2 _____

3 _____

4 _____

4 Read the following paragraph. Then discuss the questions below.

There are several differences between the cacao tree and the plant called nightshade. One difference is the places where they grow. Cacao trees grow in Central and South America. In contrast, nightshade grows in parts of Europe, Africa, Asia, and North America. The cacao tree and nightshade also look very different. The cacao tree grows about eight meters high, but nightshade grows only to about one meter. The most important difference between the cacao tree and nightshade is the fruit they produce. Cacao trees produce huge berries called cacao pods. Inside the pods are seeds that are used to make chocolate. Unlike the cacao fruit, nightshade berries are poisonous. In fact, if you eat nightshade, you could die. As you can see, nightshade and the cacao tree are two very different plants.

A cacao tree

A nightshade plant

1 What two things is the writer contrasting?

2 How many points of contrast does the writer discuss? What are they?

3 Underline all the expressions of difference.

5 Write a paragraph about the differences between two plants you know. Remember to start with a topic sentence. Include two or three differences between the plants. Use some expressions of difference that you learned in this chapter. End with a concluding sentence. Then compare your paragraph with a partner's.

Preparing to read

THINKING ABOUT THE TOPIC BEFORE YOU READ

The text you are going to read is about animals. There are many different types of animals on our planet, and scientists categorize, or group, them in a variety of ways. With a partner or in a small group, do the activities below.

1 Read the names of animals in the box below. Think about their similarities and differences.

bird	elephant	lion	spider
cow	fish	monkey	turtle
crab	kangaroo	mosquito	whale
dog	ladybug	mouse	worm

1 On a separate piece of paper, divide the animals into categories. You may use as many categories as you wish. Use a dictionary for help, if necessary.

2 Look again at the list of animals in the box. Group the animals again, but use different categories this time.

3 In a class discussion, compare the different ways you categorized the animals.

2 Look at the photographs. Notice that each one shows a relationship between two types of organisms. Then discuss the questions below in a small group.

a   b   c

1 In photograph a, what kind of relationship do you think the rhinoceros and the birds have?

2 In photograph b, what kind of relationship do you think the turtle and the fish have?

3 In photograph c, what kind of relationship do you think the mosquito and the human have?

Now read

Now read the text "Animal Life." When you finish, turn to the tasks on page 157.

3 ANIMAL LIFE

Animal life on Earth is very diverse. There are even more different kinds of animals than there are plants. Scientists have identified and named more than 1.8 million **species** of animals. They believe there are still millions more to identify in the future.

Vertebrates and invertebrates

There are two main groups of animals: vertebrates and invertebrates. Vertebrates are animals that have a backbone. A backbone is a line of bones that goes down the middle of the animal's back. It supports the animal and protects the spinal cord, which is an important group of nerves that sends messages between the brain and the rest of the body. Every vertebrate also has a head with a skull that surrounds and protects the brain. Fish, snakes, birds, and monkeys are all vertebrates.

Invertebrates are animals that do not have backbones, such as worms and spiders. About 95 percent of all animals are invertebrates. Many of them have a hard protective covering such as a shell. Invertebrates can live anywhere, but most, like the starfish and the crab, live in the ocean.

Snakes are vertebrates.

Starfish are invertebrates.

Symbiotic relationships

Animals connect with each other in various ways. One way is by forming relationships, called symbiotic relationships, with other organisms. Symbiosis is any close relationship between living things. There are three categories of symbiotic relationships: mutualism, commensalism, and parasitism.

When both organisms benefit from the relationship, it is called mutualism. For example, some small birds sit on water buffaloes and eat the insects that bother the animals. In this relationship, the bird benefits by getting food, and the water buffalo benefits by getting fewer insect bites. Commensalism is a symbiotic relationship in which one organism benefits and the other is not affected. For example, sometimes a fly lands on the back of a cow that is walking across a field. The fly benefits because it gets a ride to a new place. The cow is neither hurt nor helped by the fly. When one organism benefits and the other is hurt, the relationship is called parasitism. For example, ticks often attach themselves to the skin of other animals, such as dogs. The tick benefits because it gets food by drinking the dog's blood. However, the dog gets hurt when the tick drinks its blood, and it often gets sick.

Dangers for animals

Human activities, such as deforestation, and environmental changes, such as global warming, are dangerous for animals as well as plants. Many animal species are losing their habitats. Some are endangered (in danger of becoming extinct); others are already extinct. Many biologists and environmentalists think these changes in animal life are a clear warning about the future health of our planet.

6

Animal Communication

Can animals talk? Can they have conversations and share information? Although animals do not communicate in the same way that humans do, many have their own special languages, which they use for different purposes. For example, animals "talk" to establish relationships with other animals: They attract mates, scare away their enemies, mark their territories, and identify themselves. Many animals use several different communication techniques. Two common ones are auditory and tactile communication.

Auditory communication refers to the sounds that animals make. Coyotes, for example, are very noisy. They use barks, yips, and howls to mark their territory and to let other coyotes know where they are.

Tactile communication means using touch to show power or to form connections with others. Did you ever see a dog push another dog over on its back to show who is boss? Perhaps in a zoo, you have seen female monkeys who kiss and hug their babies. Another example is the friendly cat that rubs cheeks with other cats. These are just a few examples of how animals communicate.

After you read

Task 1 APPLYING WHAT YOU HAVE READ

1 Work with a partner. Look at the pictures below, and name all the animals you can. Then label each picture *V* (vertebrate animal) or *I* (invertebrate animal). Base your answers on the information in the text "Animal Life."

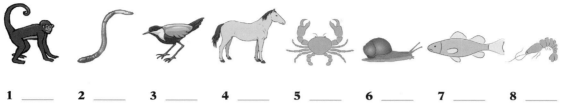

1 _____ 2 _____ 3 _____ 4 _____ 5 _____ 6 _____ 7 _____ 8 _____

2 Each situation below describes a relationship between two animals. Based on the information in the text, write *M* (mutualism), *C* (commensalism), or *P* (parasitism).

_____ **1** A shrimp digs a hole in the sand. It lives there with a goby fish. The shrimp cannot see well. If there is danger when they are outside the hole, the goby fish touches the shrimp to warn it. Both animals go back into the hole.

_____ **2** The suckerfish and the shark travel together. When the shark finds something to eat, the suckerfish also eats some of the food. This does not bother the shark.

_____ **3** A tapeworm lives inside a dog. The tapeworm is safe and eats food from the dog's intestine. The dog does not get the nutrients from the food the tapeworm eats.

_____ **4** An ant protects a butterfly from enemies. The butterfly provides food for the ant.

_____ **5** A mosquito bites a bird and drinks its blood. The mosquito needs a substance in the blood to produce eggs. The bird feels uncomfortable and sometimes gets sick from the bite.

3 Write *endangered* or *extinct* to describe the condition of each animal below. Base your answers on the information in the text.

_____ **1** Dinosaurs: These huge animals lived on Earth until about 65 million years ago. There are no dinosaurs on our planet today.

_____ **2** Siberian tigers: There are only about 400 Siberian tigers in the world today. Many have been killed, and many have lost their homes because of deforestation and building. These tigers may eventually disappear.

4 Compare your answers to steps 1–3 in a small group.

Task 2 LANGUAGE FOCUS: *THAT* CLAUSES

Remember that sentences in English can have more than one clause.
A *that* clause is one type of adjective clause. It functions the same way
as an adjective: It modifies, or describes, a noun or noun phrase. In the
examples below, each sentence has a *that* clause and a main clause. *That*
clauses always follow the nouns they modify.

main clause   adjective clause

noun phrase

A crab is an animal that has a shell.

main clause   adjective clause

noun phrase

Earth is a planet that has a lot of diverse forms of life.

1 Find and underline each sentence in the text "Animal Life" that includes a *that*
clause. Then circle the noun it modifies. Compare your answers with a partner's.

2 Complete the *that* clauses in the following sentences with your own ideas. Compare
your sentences with a partner's.

1 Plants are organisms that _____ .

2 Birds are animals that _____ .

3 Human activities cause environmental changes that _____ .

4 Some animals form relationships that _____ .

5 Earth is a planet that _____ .

Task 3 BUILDING VOCABULARY: COMPOUND WORDS

Compound words are made up of two or more words. You can often
guess the meaning of a compound word by combining the meanings of its
parts. For example, *starfish* is made up of the two words *star* and *fish*. A
starfish is an invertebrate that lives in the ocean. It is shaped like a star.

1 Guess the meanings of the compound words below. Use your knowledge of the
smaller words that make up the compound words.

1 backbone   **4** racehorse

2 jellyfish   **5** brainstorm

3 redwood tree   **6** mountaintop

2 Use the words in the box to make as many compound words as you can.

bird	earth	fall	fish	flower
quake	rain	shell	shine	storm
song	sun	thunder	water	worm

3 What other compound words do you know? With a partner, make a list of compound words and share it with the class.

Task 4 WRITING ABOUT SIMILARITIES AND DIFFERENCES

For some assignments, you will have to write about both the similarities and the differences between two or more people, places, things, or ideas. In other words, you will have to compare and contrast them. Here are some guidelines:

- Write a topic sentence that states the main idea. For example:
  X and Y are similar to and different from each other in several ways.

- Following the topic sentence, explain the similarities.

- Get ready to explain the differences. First, write a transition sentence to signal the change from the similarities to the differences. Here are two examples:
  X and Y have similarities, but they also have differences.
  Although X and Y have similarities, they also have important differences.

- Explain the differences.

- End with a concluding sentence that restates the main idea.

1 Read the following paragraph. Then, with a partner, answer the questions at the top of the next page.

> Sharks and jellyfish are similar to and different from each other in several ways. One similarity is that both animals live in the ocean. Another similarity is that both sharks and jellyfish can hurt people and other animals. A shark can bite with its sharp teeth, and a jellyfish can sting with its tentacles. Although there are similarities between these animals, there are also important differences. One difference is that sharks are vertebrates and jellyfish are invertebrates. This means that, unlike sharks, jellyfish do not have backbones or brains. Sharks and jellyfish also have different life spans. Most jellyfish live only a few months. In contrast, most sharks live 15–20 years. These facts show that sharks and jellyfish are similar and different at the same time.

1 What two things does the writer compare and contrast?

2 What are the similarities? What are the differences?

3 Underline all the expressions of similarity and difference.

2 Now write a paragraph that compares and contrasts plants and animals.

1 In a small group, brainstorm a list of similarities and differences between plants and animals. Then share your ideas with the class.

2 Choose two similarities and two differences to include in the paragraph. One way you can organize your ideas is a Venn diagram. (Review "Using a Venn Diagram" on page 125, if necessary.)

3 Now write the paragraph. Follow the guidelines in the box on page 159.

Task 5 THINKING CRITICALLY ABOUT THE TOPIC

1 Discuss the following questions with your classmates:

1 Do you know of any animals that are endangered or extinct? If so, name them.

2 Deforestation and global warming are two reasons that animals may become endangered or extinct. What are some other reasons?

2 Reread the boxed text "Animal Communication." Then discuss the following questions with a partner or in a small group:

1 Have you ever seen animals communicate with each other? If so, describe the situation.

2 What are some communication techniques that animals use? Give examples.

3 What are some ways that animals communicate with people? Give examples.

3 Look at the cartoon. What do you think is the main idea?

Frankly, I think we should stop trying to communicate with Humans: They're simply not smart enough to understand us.

Chapter 7   Writing Assignment

Write a paragraph that compares and contrasts two organisms. For example, you could write about two different animals, two different plants, or a plant and an animal. Use information from this chapter and your own ideas. Do some additional research in the library or on the Internet. Follow the steps and the guidelines below.

1 | Choose two organisms and find some information about them. Take notes on what you find.

2 | Discuss what you learned with a partner or in a small group.

3 | On your own, brainstorm a list of similarities and differences between the two organisms. One way to organize your ideas is in a Venn diagram. (See "Using a Venn Diagram" on page 125.)

4 | Review your list and choose two similarities and two differences that you want to include in the paragraph.

5 | Now write the first draft of the paragraph.

Guidelines
- Include a topic sentence and at least one supporting sentence for each similarity and each difference.
- Use a transition sentence between the similarities and the differences.
- Include any relevant vocabulary and information from this chapter.
- Use some expressions of similarity and difference (see the Language Focus tasks, pages 144 and 152) and *that* clauses as appropriate (see the Language Focus task, page 158).
- End the paragraph with a concluding sentence.
- Give the paragraph a title.

---

6 | When you finish writing, exchange paragraphs with a partner and read each other's work. Then discuss the following questions about both paragraphs:

 1 Which idea in your partner's paragraph do you think is the most interesting?

 2 Does your partner's paragraph have correct form and structure?

 3 Does the paragraph include both similarities and differences?

 4 Are all the ideas clear and in logical order?

 5 Are there any irrelevant sentences?

 6 Is there a transition sentence between the part about similarities and the part about differences?

7 | Think about any changes that would improve your paragraph. Then write a second draft.

Preparing to read

THINKING ABOUT THE TOPIC BEFORE YOU READ

1 | What do you think makes humans unique, that is, different from all other organisms? Brainstorm a list of ideas with a partner.

2 | The brain is one of the most important organs in the body. It controls almost everything we do. It even influences what we see.

Work with a partner. Describe what you see in the picture on the right.

3 | Did you and your partner see the same thing in the picture? Look again, and this time, try to find two images. If you see only one image, try looking at the picture from farther away.

4 | Discuss the images you saw in step 2 with the class. Then read the information below.

The brain is always trying to understand the world around us. For example, when our eyes send information to the brain, the brain tries to understand it by comparing that information to something we have seen before. Usually, this is easy, but sometimes it is not. For example, look at the picture on the left. Your eyes see black marks, and it is your brain's job to figure out what these marks mean. In this case, the brain has to compare the marks to two different things: a duck and a rabbit. This can take a few minutes because the brain has to switch back and forth between the idea of a duck and the idea of a rabbit, trying to decide which one the picture shows.

Now read

Now read the text "The Brain." When you finish, turn to the tasks on page 165.

The Human Body

Chapter 8

1 THE BRAIN

Just like other organisms, humans are made of cells that grow, develop, and eventually die. However, as far as we know, only humans are able to think about ideas, and only humans have a sense of self (an understanding that they are unique individuals). An important reason for these differences is the human brain. Although some animals have larger brains, the human brain is much more complex than any other. It is the center of our thoughts, actions, feelings, dreams, and memories. The brain makes it possible for us to do many things that other organisms cannot. For example, we are able to use language, make music, create art, and develop complex tools and technologies.

Composition, structure, and function

When scientists describe the brain, they note several key features. Surprisingly, the brain is quite small, even though it is complex. An average brain is about the size of two fists, and it weighs approximately 1.4 kilograms. Some people describe the brain as looking like a soft, pink, wrinkled rock. Others say it looks like a sponge. This important organ consists of three parts: the cerebrum, the cerebellum, and the brain stem.

cerebrum

the part of the brain that controls thinking, learning, language, memory, feelings, and personality

cerebellum

the part of the brain that controls movement of the body

brain stem

the part of the brain that controls basic functions, such as breathing, sleeping, body temperature, and the heartbeat

The **cerebrum** is the largest part of the brain. It controls most of 3 our thinking, speaking, and our five senses: sight, hearing, touch, taste, and smell. The cerebrum is divided into two halves, or hemispheres. The left hemisphere is important for speech, language, logic, and math skills. The right hemisphere is important for creative abilities, such as playing music, drawing, painting, and writing books. Some people seem to use one hemisphere a little more than the other. For example, a concert pianist might use the right hemisphere more. A mathematician might use the left hemisphere more. However, in the human brain, the two hemispheres work together, so that we are able to do a wide variety of things.

The **cerebellum** controls the body's movements, balance, and 4 muscle coordination (the way the muscles work together). The **brain stem** is the smallest part of the brain. It connects the brain to the spinal cord and the rest of the body. It controls some of the body's basic functions, such as the heartbeat and breathing. It also handles all the messages between the brain and the body.

The processing of messages

Every second of your life, your brain receives 5 messages from the parts of your body and the world around you. The brain interprets, or figures out, these messages, and it tells you what to think and how to act. For example, if you drop a book on your foot, it is your brain, not your foot, that tells you what happened and what to do about it. Similarly, your eyes send messages to the brain, and the brain tells you what you see. In this way, the brain controls almost everything you do.

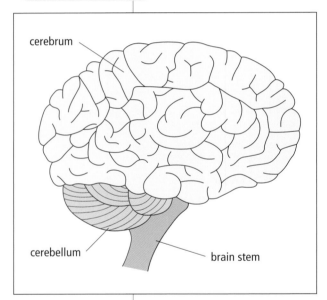

Figure 8.1
The brain

Brain research

The brain is still a mystery, but scientists are 6 learning more about it all the time. For example, some medical researchers are learning how to improve the treatment of brain injuries, diseases, and disabilities, such as Alzheimer's disease and autism. Others are experimenting with implanting computer chips in the brain to help paralyzed people move again. In education, some brain researchers are applying their knowledge to the classroom. They are helping students and teachers to learn and to teach more effectively. Because of advances like these, many scientists consider brain research to be one of the most interesting and exciting areas for future study.

After you read

Task 1 NOTE TAKING: FROM HIGHLIGHTING TO NOTES

> Highlighting important information in a text is a helpful first step in taking notes.
>
> • First, read the text all the way through without highlighting.
> • Read the text a second time. As you read, highlight the main points and supporting details. Do not highlight every sentence. A text with more than half of the sentences highlighted is not useful.
> • If possible, use different colors as you highlight. One way is to highlight the main points in one color and the supporting details in a different color.
> • Review the material you have highlighted. Make notes in the margin to help you remember why the highlighted information is important.

1 Below is paragraph 6 from the text "The Brain." Look at how one student highlighted the information. Then, with a partner, discuss the questions below the paragraph.

---

brain injuries, diseases, + disabilities

computer-chip implants

The brain is still a mystery, but scientists are learning more about it all the time. For example, some medical researchers are learning how to improve the treatment of brain injuries, diseases, and disabilities, such as Alzheimer's disease and autism. Others are experimenting with implanting computer chips in the brain to help paralyzed people move again. In education, some brain researchers are applying their knowledge to the classroom. They are helping students and teachers to learn and to teach more effectively. Because of advances like these, many scientists consider brain research to be one of the most interesting and exciting areas for future study.

brain research

better learning + teaching

---

1 Which highlighted idea is the main idea, and which ideas are details?

2 Do you agree with the way the student highlighted the text? Would you have highlighted any part of it differently?

3 Are the notes in the margin clear to you? Would you have written any of the notes differently? If so, which notes would you change?

2 Reread paragraphs 1–5 of the text "The Brain," and highlight the main ideas and supporting details. Then make notes in the margin about the information you highlighted. You may find that some paragraphs have more than one main idea.

3 Compare your work with your partner's.

Task 2 BUILDING VOCABULARY: USING ADJECTIVES

Adjectives add both information and interest to a text by giving more details. For example, compare these two sentences:

- The brain looks like a rock.
- The brain looks like a **soft, pink, wrinkled** rock.

The first sentence above is factual, but the second sentence gives more information, and it provides the reader with a better picture of the brain.

Be careful! Do not use too many adjectives. If a sentence or text has too many adjectives, it can be hard to read and understand.

1 Read the text below about a man named Phineas Gage. Underline the adjectives. Notice how they add information about the man and make the text more interesting.

> Phineas Gage was a railroad employee. He was a good worker and a respected man. His employer thought he was smart and responsible, and the people he supervised said he was a fair boss. One day in 1848, there was a terrible accident. A heavy iron bar went right through Gage's head. He did not die, but a large section of the front part of his brain was destroyed.
>
> When Gage went back to work the next year, everyone noticed enormous changes in his personality. Before the accident, Gage was calm, hardworking, responsible, and friendly. However, after the accident, he became angry, childish, rude, and impatient. Years later, scientists discovered that the front part of the brain controls personality. This explains why Gage's personality changed so much after his injury.

2 On a separate piece of paper, rewrite the sentences below, adding one or two appropriate adjectives to each one.

1 The brain is an organ.
2 Humans have brains.
3 There are plants on Earth.
4 Mosquitoes are insects.
5 Elephants are animals.

3 Write a few sentences that describe an organism, but do not use the name of the organism in your description. Use some adjectives to make the description clear and interesting.

4 Read your sentences from step 3 to a partner. Try to guess what organism your partner's sentences describe. Then have your partner do the same.

Task 3 LANGUAGE FOCUS: GERUNDS

A gerund is an *-ing* form of a verb that is used as a noun. A gerund can be the subject of a sentence or the object of a verb.

gerund as subject

Exercising is one way to keep your body healthy.

verb   gerund as object of verb

I really **like** **exercising**.

Be careful! Not all *-ing* forms are gerunds. Some are used as verbs, and it is important to recognize the difference so that you can understand what you read.

-ing form as verb

We **are exercising** in the gym for one hour today.

1 Read the sentences below. Underline the words that end in *-ing*. Then decide if the *-ing* form is used as a noun or a verb. If it is a noun, write *G* (gerund) next to the sentence.

_____ **1** Thinking is something our brains do all day long.

_____ **2** Many scientists are doing brain research.

_____ **3** Experts say sleeping is very important for healthy brain development.

_____ **4** Hearing and seeing are two senses that the brain controls.

_____ **5** Scientists are learning more about the brain every day.

2 Complete each of the following sentences with an appropriate gerund. Base your answers on the information in the text "The Brain."

1 The cerebrum controls most of a person's _____ and _____ .

2 The right hemisphere of the brain is important for creative abilities, such as _____ and _____ .

3 The brain stem controls some of the body's basic functions, such as _____ .

3 Work with a partner. Take turns asking and answering questions using gerunds. For example, you could ask about places (*visit*), food (*eat*), clothes (*wear*), movies (*watch*), music (*listen*), and holidays (*celebrate*).

Which _____ do you enjoy _____-ing?
Which places do you enjoy visiting?

Task 4 APPLYING WHAT YOU HAVE READ

Today many scientists and educators believe that the right and left hemispheres affect the strategies that different people use to learn new information. Reread paragraph 3 of the text "The Brain." Then do the following activity.

1 Read the sentences below. Write a check (✔) next to each sentence that describes you.

_____ **1** I always look at the clock, and I like to wear a watch.

_____ **2** Before I make a difficult decision, I write down the pros (advantages) and the cons (disadvantages).

_____ **3** I often change my plans. I don't like to follow a schedule.

_____ **4** When someone asks me for directions, I like to draw a map. I think it's easier than using words to explain how to get somewhere.

_____ **5** I learn math easily.

_____ **6** I like to draw.

_____ **7** People tell me I'm always late.

_____ **8** I learn music easily.

_____ **9** I like to have a "to-do" list.

_____ **10** I read the directions before putting something together, such as a piece of furniture or electronic equipment.

2 Now look at the key at the bottom of this page. Next to each sentence you checked, write either *L* (left hemisphere) or *R* (right hemisphere), according to the key.

3 Count how many *L*s and *R*s you checked. Then read the information below to find out how your answers match with learning strategies that might work well for you.

> If you checked more *L*s, then you may use the left half of your brain a little more than the right half. In that case, the following learning strategies might work for you:
> - Study in a quiet place.
> - Work independently, not with other people.
> - Memorize new words and information.
>
> If you checked more *R*s, you may use the right half of your brain a little more than the left half. In that case, the following learning strategies might work for you:
> - Work in groups.
> - Draw pictures to support your notes.
> - Do hands-on activities, such as conducting surveys and doing experiments.
>
> If you checked the same number of *L*s and *R*s, you probably use both halves of your brain equally. In that case, using a variety of learning strategies might work best for you.

Key for step 2: **1** L, **2** L, **3** R, **4** R, **5** L, **6** R, **7** R, **8** R, **9** L, **10** L

Task 5 WRITING A DESCRIPTION

For some academic assignments, you will have to write a description. For example, in science classes, you may need to describe a landform, a plant, an animal, or a part of the body. A good description includes specific details about the topic. Think about including details of appearance, such as height, weight, color, shape, and size. Use adjectives and measurements where appropriate. Use words that will create a picture for the reader.

1 | Read the following description from the text "The Brain," and answer the questions below.

> When scientists describe the brain, they note several key features. Surprisingly, the brain is quite small, even though it is complex. An average brain is about the size of two fists, and it weighs approximately 1.4 kilograms. Some people describe the brain as looking like a soft, pink, wrinkled rock. Others say it looks like a sponge. This important organ consists of three parts: the cerebrum, the cerebellum, and the brain stem.

1 What is the writer describing?

2 Circle the adjectives that make the description clearer.

3 Underline the other details that help you "see" what the writer is describing.

2 | Look at your eyes in a mirror. Then look at the eyes of some of your classmates. What do they look like? Think about their shape, color, size, and any other details that help describe them. Write some notes about the eye on a separate piece of paper.

3 | Now write a paragraph that describes the human eye. Write as many specific details as you can. Include adjectives and measurements where appropriate.

4 | Draw a picture of an eye to go along with your description.

5 | Compare your paragraph with a partner's.

Preparing to read

THINKING ABOUT THE TOPIC BEFORE YOU READ

How much do you know about the bones and muscles in the human body? Work with a partner, and answer the questions below. You will be able to check your answers when you read the text "The Skeletal and Muscular Systems."

1 Look at the pictures below. Which one shows the skeletal (bone) system? Which one shows the muscular system? Label each picture with the name of the appropriate system.

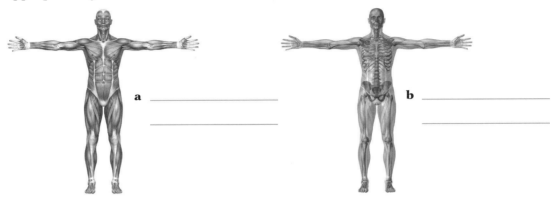

a _____

_____

b _____

_____

2 Read each sentence below. Write *B* if you think the sentence is about bones, *M* if you think it is about muscles, and *B/M* if you think it is about both bones and muscles.

_____ **1** are hard on the outside

_____ **2** need exercise and a good diet to stay healthy

_____ **3** help you digest food

_____ **4** are made of cells

_____ **5** can get shorter

_____ **6** (some) protect the body's organs

3 Circle the correct word or number in the parentheses.

1 There are (123 / 206 / 390) bones in the human body.

2 The human body has (more muscles than bones / more bones than muscles).

3 The longest bone in the body is the (backbone / thighbone / rib).

4 You (can / cannot) control all the muscles in your body.

Now read

Now read the text "The Skeletal and Muscular Systems." When you finish, turn to the tasks on page 173.

2 THE SKELETAL AND MUSCULAR SYSTEMS

In just one day, our bodies move in thousands of ways, and we make [1] some of those movements over and over. For example, we walk an average of 5,000 steps every day, and we usually bend our bodies 200–400 times a day. Some of our movements are unconscious, that is, we do not think about them. For instance, we normally blink our eyes over 10,000 times a day. If we did not have both bones and muscles, we would not be able to walk, talk, sit, bend, blink, or smile. In fact, we would not be able to move at all.

Bones

Inside the body is a framework of 206 bones, called a **skeleton**. Bones [2] are made of living cells and tissue, and they give shape and support to the body. They are both lightweight and strong. The outside of a bone is hard and solid, and the inside has some empty spaces, which makes it light. An average skeleton weighs only about 10 kilograms, but it is strong enough to support the body and hold it upright.

skeleton
a frame of bones that supports the body

Bones have two main purposes. Some [3] bones protect the internal organs. For example, the skull bones protect the brain, the ribs protect the heart, and the backbone protects the spinal cord. Other bones, such as the femur, or thighbone, help support the body. The femur is the longest bone in the body. It is an average of 48 centimeters long, and it supports the weight of the body as we walk and run.

Muscles

Muscles are also made of cells, but they are [4] very different from bones. Muscles allow the body to move by contracting and relaxing. When a muscle contracts, it gets shorter and tighter. Some muscles contract and relax automatically. These muscles are called involuntary muscles, and we cannot control them. For example, the stomach muscles contract and relax to digest food, and the cardiac muscle in the heart contracts and relaxes each time the heart beats.

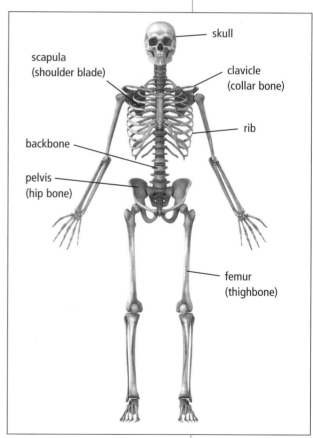

Figure 8.2 Major bones in the body

Muscles that we can control are called voluntary muscles, or skeletal [5] muscles. There are over 600 of these muscles attached to the skeleton. They control every movement we make by pulling on the bones they are attached to. For example, the biceps and triceps muscles in our arms and the hamstring and quadriceps muscles in our legs are the major muscles that help us walk or pick things up. However, in order to move, we also need all the smaller muscles that work with the major muscles. In fact, it takes hundreds of muscles to take one step, 43 muscles to frown, and 17 muscles to smile.

Bone and muscle health

You probably do not think about your bones and muscles when you walk, talk, run, and smile. In fact, you probably take these parts of your body for granted unless they become injured. However, it is very important to keep bones and muscles strong by exercising regularly and eating a healthy diet. If you take good care of your skeletal and muscular systems, you will enjoy the movement and strength they provide for many years to come.

6

Jogging is one way to keep bones and muscles strong.

Facts about Bones and Muscles in the Human Body

- Babies are born with about 300 bones, and as they grow, some of the bones join together. That's why adults have only 206 bones.
- More than 50 percent of the bones in the body are in the hands and feet. There are 27 bones in each hand and 26 bones in each foot.
- Water makes up about 25 percent of the content of bones.
- The smallest bone in the body is inside the ear. It is the stirrup bone, and it is approximately .28 centimeters long.
- The body has more than 600 muscles, and they make up 35–45 percent of a person's body weight.

After you read

Task 1 ASKING AND ANSWERING QUESTIONS ABOUT A TEXT

Remember that asking and answering questions about a text is a good way to make sure you have understood what you read.

1| With a partner, take turns answering the following questions about paragraphs 1–3 of the text "The Skeletal and Muscular Systems."

   1 What are some ways our bodies move every day?

   2 What parts of the body allow us to move in so many ways?

   3 What is a skeleton? Why is it important?

   4 Describe a bone.

   5 What are the two main purposes of bones?

   6 Give one example of a bone and explain its purpose.

2| With your partner, take turns asking and answering questions about paragraphs 4–6 of the text.

Task 2 NOTE TAKING: FROM HIGHLIGHTING TO NOTES

Highlighting and writing margin notes are useful strategies that focus your attention on important information in a text and help you remember it. It is often even more effective to use a separate piece of paper to write more detailed notes based on your highlighting.

1| Go back to the text "The Skeletal and Muscular Systems," and highlight the main ideas and important supporting details in paragraph 3. If possible, use one color for the main ideas and a different color for the details. Make notes in the margin about the information you highlighted.

2| Review "Note Taking: From Highlighting to Notes" on page 165. Then, on a separate piece of paper, write more detailed notes, basing them on your highlighting and margin notes.

3| Compare your notes with a partner's.

4| Choose another paragraph in the text. Highlight and take notes on the main ideas and important details.

Task 3 SCANNING FOR DETAILS

Scan the text "The Skeletal and Muscular Systems" to find the following information. Remember not to read every word. Just look for the information you need.

1 How many steps do people usually take in one day?

2 How many bones does your body have?

3 How much does an average human skeleton weigh?

4 Which is the longest bone in the body? How long is it?

5 How many skeletal muscles does your body have?

6 Does it take more muscles to smile or to frown?

7 How many bones do babies have? How many bones do adults have?

8 Where are half of the bones in the body located?

Task 4 BUILDING VOCABULARY: USING A DICTIONARY

The sentences below are from the text "The Skeletal and Muscular Systems." In each sentence, the word in **bold** has more than one meaning. Use your dictionary and the context of the sentence to choose the correct part of speech and definition for each word.

1 For example, we walk an average of 5,000 **steps** every day.

Correct definition: _____

2 Bones are made of living cells and **tissue**, and they give shape and support to the body.

Correct definition: _____

3 Some muscles **contract** and relax automatically.

Correct definition: _____

4 Some muscles contract and **relax** automatically.

Correct definition: _____

5 However, in order to move, we also need all the smaller muscles that work with the **major** muscles.

Correct definition: _____

6 However, it is very important to keep bones and muscles strong by exercising regularly and eating a healthy **diet**.

Correct definition: _____

Task 5 BUILDING VOCABULARY: WORDS THAT CAN BE USED AS NOUNS OR VERBS

> English has many words that can be used as either nouns or verbs. Learning both uses of these words will help you increase your vocabulary.

1 The sentences below are based on the text "The Skeletal and Muscular Systems." They show how the words in **bold** can be used as either nouns or verbs:

- Bones give **shape** (*n.*) to the body.
  Bones **shape** (*v.*) the body.
- A **smile** (*n.*) uses 17 muscles.
  It takes 17 muscles to **smile** (*v.*).

2 In the sentences below, the words in bold are nouns, but they can also be used as verbs. Rewrite each sentence, using the word in bold as a verb.

1 The femur gives **support** to the body when we run.

_____.

2 Doctors listen to the **beat** of a patient's heart to make sure it is healthy.

_____.

3 Choose two words from the box below. Look back at the text to see how the words you chose are used. You can also look them up in a dictionary. On a separate piece of paper, write two sentences for each word. In one sentence, use the word as a noun. In the other sentence, use the word as a verb.

| control   frown   walk   work |

Task 6 WRITING A DESCRIPTION

> Remember that descriptive writing includes adjectives and measurements to explain in detail what something looks and feels like. Descriptions may provide information about size, color, shape, and weight.

1 Look back at the text "The Skeletal and Muscular Systems." Which paragraphs include descriptive writing? What does each of those paragraphs describe? Underline the descriptive words and information.

2 In small groups, describe your hand. What does it look like? What color is it? How big is it? What adjectives would you use to describe it? Take notes on your discussion.

3 Write a paragraph describing your hand.

Preparing to read

BUILDING BACKGROUND KNOWLEDGE ABOUT THE TOPIC

1 | Read the following information about the circulatory system.

> Blood is always circulating, or moving, through the heart and around the body. It is part of the circulatory system, which transports materials to and from all the cells. The other two parts of this system are the heart and the blood vessels. The heart pumps, or pushes, the blood through the body. When blood leaves the heart, it travels through small tubes, called blood vessels. The blood delivers oxygen, water, and nutrients to all of the body's cells. On the trip back to the heart, the blood picks up waste products, such as carbon dioxide, so that the body can get rid of them. This circulating supply of blood keeps the body working well.

2 | Answer the following questions with a partner:

1 What does the circulatory system do?

2 Name the three main parts of the circulatory system. What does each part do?

CONDUCTING AN EXPERIMENT

> In science classes, you will often conduct experiments. An experiment is a hands-on way to find out or to test information.

With each beat of the heart, the blood moves through the body. You can feel the blood moving at pulse points, such as the neck and the wrist. Find out how fast your heart is beating. Follow the steps below.

1 Hold one hand in front of you. Place the first two fingers of your other hand on the inside of your wrist, and feel for your pulse.

2 When you find your pulse, count how many beats you feel in 15 seconds. Multiply this number by 4. The result is your pulse rate per minute. Record your pulse rate: _____

3 When you move quickly, your body needs more oxygen-filled blood than when you are resting. This means your heart must pump faster. Run in place for one minute and take your pulse again. Record your pulse rate now: _____

Now read

Now read the text "The Heart and the Circulatory System." When you finish, turn to the tasks on page 179.

3 THE HEART AND THE CIRCULATORY SYSTEM

The heart is only about the size of a fist, but it is the most important muscle in the body. It weighs about 300 grams, and it is mostly red, just like other muscles. The heart normally pumps, or beats, between 60 and 100 times a minute, and it delivers more than 7,500 liters of blood each day to all the cells in the body. On average, the heart beats approximately 100,000 times a day and about 2.5 billion times in a lifetime.

Features of the circulatory system

The heart is the center of the **circulatory system**, which also includes blood vessels and blood. The circulatory system is the body's internal transportation system. Blood travels through small tubes called blood vessels to all parts of the body, carrying the gases, water, and nutrients that people need to live and stay healthy.

Every time the heart beats, it pushes blood through the body's blood vessels. There are more than 96,000 kilometers of blood vessels inside the body. If they were stretched out, they would circle Earth more than two times. Arteries are blood vessels that carry blood away from the heart to all parts of the body. Veins are blood vessels that carry blood from the body back to the heart. Arteries and veins are connected by tiny blood vessels called capillaries.

The flow of blood through the heart

The heart is divided in half, and each half has two chambers. The four chambers hold blood that is entering and leaving the heart. The flow of blood works in this way: Blood from all over the body enters the heart through the top right chamber, called the right atrium. This blood flows to the bottom right chamber, called the right ventricle. The heart then pumps the blood out of the right ventricle, through the pulmonary artery, into the lungs.

In the lungs, the blood picks up oxygen, and then it returns to the heart through the left atrium. Next, the blood flows to the left ventricle. The heart then pumps the blood out of the left ventricle into the aorta, which is the largest artery in the body. The blood travels through the aorta and other smaller arteries to all parts of the body, delivering oxygen to all the cells. The blood then travels through capillaries to veins that lead back to the heart. From the veins,

1

2 **circulatory system**
the system that carries food and gases to the cells of the body

3

4

Figure 8.3 The flow of blood through the heart

5

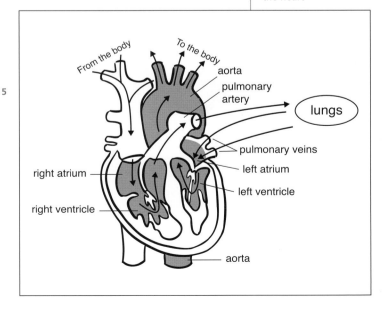

the blood goes into the right atrium of the heart to begin the process again. The whole cycle takes about 30 seconds.

Heart health

Your heart works hard. It started beating before you were born, and it will continue to beat for your whole life. Having a healthy heart means that the heart muscle is strong and that the arteries are clean and open. If the arteries that supply blood to the heart become blocked, it can cause a heart attack. Each year, millions of people die of heart attacks. Therefore, it is very important to keep your heart healthy. One of the best things you can do is to avoid smoking. Exercise and a good diet can also help keep the heart in good shape.

6

Dr. Christiaan Barnard and the First Human Heart Transplant

Louis Washkansky, a 55-year-old man in South Africa, knew he was dying. His heart was failing, and his doctors could not help him. On December 3, 1967, Dr. Christiaan Barnard performed the first human heart transplant at Groote Schuur Hospital in Cape Town. After the nine-hour operation, Mr. Washkansky had a new heart. He had to take medicine so that his body would not reject the new heart. Unfortunately, the medicine weakened his immune system, and he died from a lung disease 18 days after the transplant surgery.

Although Mr. Washkansky did not live long after his operation, Dr. Barnard had proved that heart transplants were possible, and he became famous around the world. He continued to perform heart transplants, and he tried to help his patients live longer lives after the operation. In fact, one patient lived for 24 years after her heart transplant in 1969.

In the 1980s, scientists developed better medicines to give patients after their heart operations. As a result, today many patients live long and healthy lives after transplant surgery.

Dr. Christiaan Barnard

After you read

Task 1 TEST TAKING: ANSWERING MULTIPLE CHOICE QUESTIONS

Review the strategies for answering multiple choice questions on pages 21 and 61. Then answer the questions below based on information in the text "The Heart and the Circulatory System." When you finish, compare your answers with a partner.

1 Which sentence is not true?
  a The heart is a muscle.
  b The heart normally beats between 60 and 100 times an hour.
  c The heart pumps blood through the whole body.
  d The heart beats billions of times in a lifetime.

2 _____ is not part of the circulatory system.
  a The heart
  b A blood vessel
  c Blood
  d The femur

3 _____ is not a blood vessel.
  a An artery
  b A vein
  c A capillary
  d The heart

4 The largest artery is the _____.
  a vein
  b aorta
  c lung
  d right atrium

5 The blood is in the _____ before it goes to the lungs.
  a right ventricle
  b right atrium
  c left ventricle
  d left atrium

6 Blood gets oxygen in the _____.
  a left ventricle
  b aorta
  c right ventricle
  d lungs

7 One whole cycle of blood flow through the heart takes _____.
  a seconds
  b minutes
  c hours
  d days

8 _____ is healthy for the heart.
  a A heart attack
  b Smoking
  c Exercise
  d A bad diet

9 Which sentence is not true?
  a The circulatory system is the body's internal transportation system.
  b Each half of the heart has two chambers.
  c Your heart starts beating when you are born.
  d Millions of people die of heart attacks in the world each year.

10 Dr. Barnard proved that _____.
  a arteries can become blocked
  b heart transplants are possible
  c lung disease always follows heart surgery
  d people cannot live long after heart surgery

Task 2 SEQUENCING

1 Review paragraphs 4 and 5 of the text "The Heart and the Circulatory System" and Figure 8.3. Then, with a partner, number the following steps of the circulatory system in the correct order (1–7).

_____ Blood flows to the left ventricle.

_____ Blood returns to the heart through the right atrium.

_____ Blood flows to the right ventricle.

_____ Blood travels through the pulmonary artery to the lungs.

___1___ Blood enters the heart through the right atrium.

_____ Blood travels through the aorta to all parts of the body.

_____ Blood picks up oxygen and returns to the heart through the left atrium.

2 Complete the diagram on the right. Draw arrows to show the path blood takes as it travels through the heart.

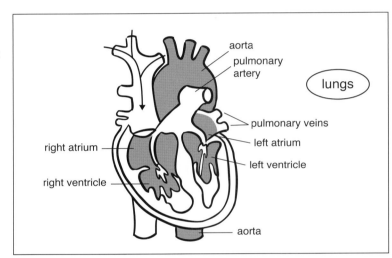

3 Look back at Figure 8.3 on page 177 to check your work.

Task 3 NOTE TAKING: FROM HIGHLIGHTING TO OUTLINING

1 Look back at the text "The Heart and the Circulatory System," and highlight the main ideas and supporting details in paragraph 3. Write short notes in the margin about the information you highlighted.

2 Below is an incomplete outline of part of the text. First, review "Note Taking: Outlining" on page 149. Then complete the outline, based on the information you highlighted and noted for paragraph 3 in step 1.

> III. *Blood vessels*
>   A. *Arteries:* _____
>   B. _____
>   C. _____

3 Now highlight the important information in paragraph 6 and make notes in the margin. Organize your highlights and notes in outline form. Start your outline this way:

> VI. Heart health
> A. Healthy heart = _____.

4 Compare your outlines in steps 2 and 3 with a partner.

Task 4 LANGUAGE FOCUS: PREPOSITIONS OF DIRECTION

Prepositions of direction show movement from one place to another. Some common prepositions of direction are *from, to, out of, into,* and *through*.

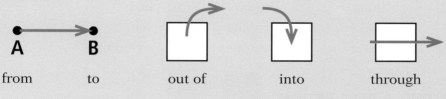

from   to   out of   into   through

Veins carry blood **from** the body **to** the heart.
Blood moves **out of** the right atrium **into** the right ventricle.
Blood travels **through** the pulmonary artery **to** the lungs.

1 Look back at paragraphs 4 and 5 of the text "The Heart and the Circulatory System." Underline all the prepositions of direction. Compare your answers with a partner's.

2 Read the sentences below. Fill in each blank with the correct preposition of direction. Base your answers on the information in the text.

1 Arteries carry blood away _____ the heart _____ all parts of the body.

2 Blood travels _____ blood vessels.

3 Blood carries oxygen _____ the lungs _____ all the cells in the body.

4 Dr. Barnard transplanted a new heart _____ the body of Louis Washkansky.

5 Blood travels _____ capillaries _____ veins.

6 The heart pumps blood _____ the left ventricle and _____ the aorta.

3 Write three sentences about other parts of the human body, such as the brain, lungs, eyes, or ears. Use at least one preposition of direction in each sentence.

1 _The brain receives messages from the body through the spinal cord._

2 _____

3 _____

4 _____

Task 5 BUILDING VOCABULARY: HAVING FUN WITH WORDS

Look at the words in the rows below. One word in each row does not belong there. Work with a partner. Decide which word in each row does not belong and explain why.

1 bones	heart	blood vessels	blood
2 gases	water	nutrients	lungs
3 right atrium	left ventricle	aorta	left atrium
4 heart	lung	brain	body
5 artery	blood	capillary	vein
6 smoking	good diet	running	swimming

Task 6 WRITING A DESCRIPTION

1 Look back at the text "The Heart and the Circulatory System" and Figure 8.3. Fill in the chart below with notes about the human heart.

Key features of the heart	Notes
size	
weight	
color	
main parts	

2 Use your notes from the chart to write a descriptive paragraph about the heart.

Chapter 8   Writing Assignment

Write a paragraph that describes the human liver. Use the facts and the diagram below. Do additional research in the library or on the Internet, and take notes on what you find. Follow the steps and the guidelines below.

1 Look at the picture and read the facts in the box. Based on your research, fill in the missing information.

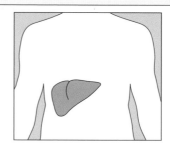

Facts about the human liver
- about the size of a football
- weighs about _____
- located below the heart
- color is _____
- feels soft
- consists of _____ main parts, called lobes

2 Compare your facts and your notes in small groups.

3 Now write the first draft of the paragraph.

Guidelines
- Include a topic sentence, supporting sentences, and a concluding sentence.
- Include vocabulary and information from this chapter and your research.
- Use adjectives and details where appropriate (see the Building Vocabulary task, page 166, and "Writing a Description," pages 169 and 182).
- Give your paragraph a title.

4 When you finish writing, exchange paragraphs with a partner and read each other's work. Then discuss the following questions about both paragraphs.

1 Which adjectives and details in your partner's paragraph helped to create a good picture of the liver?

2 Does your partner's paragraph have correct form and structure?

3 Are all the sentences relevant to the topic?

4 Are all the ideas presented in a logical order?

5 Think about any changes to your paragraph that would improve it. Then write a second draft of the paragraph.

Preparing to read

EXAMINING GRAPHIC MATERIAL

1 | Look at the graph on the right.* It is called a *bar graph* because it uses bars to show statistics.

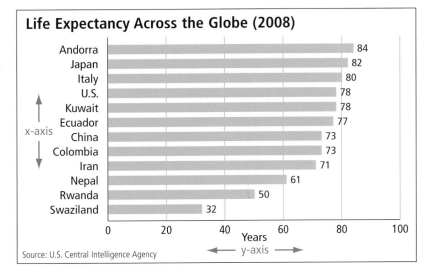

Life Expectancy Across the Globe (2008)

Country	Years
Andorra	84
Japan	82
Italy	80
U.S.	78
Kuwait	78
Ecuador	77
China	73
Colombia	73
Iran	71
Nepal	61
Rwanda	50
Swaziland	32

x-axis

Years

y-axis

Source: U.S. Central Intelligence Agency

2 | Use the graph to answer the following questions with a partner:

1 What information does the x-axis show? What information does the y-axis show?

2 What do you think *life expectancy* means?

3 How many years would a baby born in China in 2008 probably live?

4 Which country had the highest life expectancy in 2008?

5 Which country had the lowest life expectancy?

6 Did any information in the graph surprise you? Explain your answer.

THINKING ABOUT THE TOPIC BEFORE YOU READ

Discuss the following questions in a small group:

1 Why do you think life expectancy is higher in some countries and lower in others?

2 The graph shows data, or information, for just a sample of countries. What do you think the average life expectancy for the whole world was in 2008?

3 What do you think average life expectancy for the world will be in 2050? Explain your answer.

Now read

Now read the text "Life Expectancy: From 25 to 100+." When you finish, turn to the tasks on page 187.

* You can find the countries listed on the graph on the map of the world on pages 210–211.

Living Longer, Living Better?

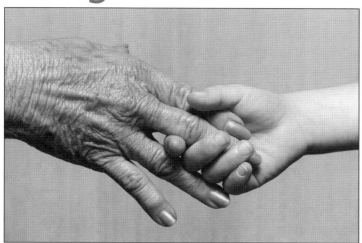

1 LIFE EXPECTANCY: FROM 25 TO 100+

In ancient and medieval times, many people did not live long. In fact, large numbers of people died as infants or children. This made the average life expectancy very low, about 25 years. By 1900, the average life expectancy was 30 years, and by 2008 it was 66 years. This data shows that for thousands of years, life expectancy around the world was relatively low. Then, suddenly, it more than doubled. How did such a huge change happen in just over 100 years?

Sanitation

Until the late nineteenth century, living conditions in much of the world were unsanitary, or very dirty. People threw garbage and waste into the streets, which usually **contaminated** the water supply. In addition, people did not have clean personal habits. They did not often wash their hands or bathe. Even doctors did not wash before seeing patients or performing operations. This lack of sanitation (cleanliness) caused diseases to spread quickly and frequently. Many people died at a young age.

Today we know there is a direct connection between sanitation and the prevention of diseases. In most places in the world, sewage systems carry waste away from houses and streets. More people understand the importance of keeping clean, at home, in public, and in doctor's offices and hospitals. As a result, more people have access to cleaner water and food, cleaner medical practices, and a generally healthier environment. These improvements in sanitation caused life expectancy to rise rapidly in the twentieth century.

contaminate
to make something, such as food or water, dangerous to use, eat, or drink

185

Nutrition

Another reason for low life expectancy was poor nutrition. In the past, people ate only the crops they could grow and the animals they could raise or catch. In addition, people could not store food for a long time, so the food they ate depended on the season. For these reasons, people did not always eat a balanced diet, and they often lacked important nutrients. This left them weaker and more likely to get sick.

4

In many parts of the world today, nutrition has improved because of better food storage and better transportation. For example, refrigeration allows people to store basic nutritious foods, such as milk, eggs, meat, and fish, for longer periods of time. In addition, ships and planes can easily carry food across countries and around the world, so that more people can eat a better variety of food all year, wherever they live. We also know more about the nutrients our bodies need. As a result, many people eat more balanced diets, including fresh fruits and vegetables, meat, fish, and grains. People are generally healthier, and they are living longer.

5

A healthier way of life

Life expectancy also depends on people's work environments and their personal habits. More people around the world have safer, cleaner working conditions than in the past, and they are working fewer hours. Studies show that not smoking is also an important way to protect health. In addition, we understand that regular exercise, rest, and stress management contribute to good health. All of these factors help explain why life expectancy has risen so dramatically in many countries, and why it may continue to increase. In fact, some experts predict that life expectancy in the future may be higher than 100 years.

6

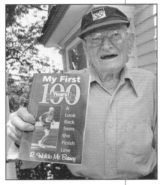

R. Waldo McBurney

Figure 9.1

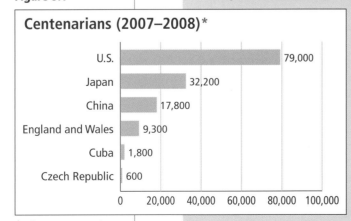

Centenarians (2007–2008)*

U.S.	79,000
Japan	32,200
China	17,800
England and Wales	9,300
Cuba	1,800
Czech Republic	600

0   20,000   40,000   60,000   80,000   100,000

* These are approximate numbers from various news sources.

R. Waldo McBurney, Centenarian

R. Waldo McBurney is an active man. Every morning, he drives to his job as a beekeeper. He enjoys running, and he has won many races. In 2004, he even wrote a book. In 2006, he celebrated his 104th birthday.

Mr. McBurney is a centenarian, a person who is a hundred years old or older. He is not alone. In 2007, there were almost 300,000 centenarians in the world, and researchers estimate that there will be 3.7 million of them in 2050. Is there a secret to living so long?

A healthy lifestyle contributes a great deal to long life. Mr. McBurney does not smoke. He exercises regularly, and he eats a healthy diet. He also has a positive attitude and a good sense of humor.

After you read

Task 1 READING FOR MAIN IDEAS AND DETAILS

1 Read each sentence below and decide if it is a main idea or a detail in the text "Life Expectancy." Write the correct letter in the blank next to each sentence.

M = a main idea in the text
D = a detail in the text

_____ **1** A healthy way of life helps people live longer.

_____ **2** In the past, people got sick because they could not always eat a balanced diet.

_____ **3** Exercising and managing stress help people live healthier lives.

_____ **4** Life expectancy has increased very quickly in the past 100 years for three reasons.

_____ **5** Smoking can reduce the number of years people live.

_____ **6** Life expectancy in the world increased as living conditions became cleaner.

_____ **7** Dirty living conditions can lead to the spread of diseases.

_____ **8** Food storage practices, such as refrigeration, help people eat better all year.

_____ **9** Better nutrition is one reason life expectancy has increased.

_____ **10** Most people today live in a cleaner environment than in the past.

2 Look back at the sentences in step 1. One of them is the main idea of the whole text.

Write it here: _____

3 Now use the sentences in step 1 to complete the chart below. First, write the sentences that express the three main ideas in the text. Then add the supporting details for each main idea.

Main ideas	Supporting details

4 Add one or two more supporting details from the text for each of the main ideas in the chart.

Task 2 APPLYING WHAT YOU HAVE READ

1 Based on the information in the text "Life Expectancy," check the habits below that can help you live a healthier and longer life.

_____ **1** eating a wide variety of foods   _____ **6** washing your hands

_____ **2** living in a place with a sewage system   _____ **7** running or jogging

_____ **3** smoking   _____ **8** eating only rice and meat

_____ **4** eating fruits and vegetables   _____ **9** playing basketball

_____ **5** working 70 hours a week   _____ **10** bathing in a dirty river

2 Discuss the following questions in a small group:

1 Name at least three more healthy habits and three more unhealthy habits.

2 Who is the healthiest person you know? Explain your answer.

3 Which healthy habits do you practice regularly?

4 Do you think you are generally a healthy person? Why or why not?

3 Explain to the class which group member has the healthiest way of life and why.

Task 3 BUILDING VOCABULARY: SUFFIXES

Remember that when you add *-ment*, or *-ion* / *-ation* to a verb, the word becomes a noun. The suffix *-age* works the same way.

move / move**ment**   protect / protec**tion**
inform / inform**ation**   store / stor**age**

When you add *-al* or *-ous* / *-ious* to a noun, the word becomes an adjective.

person / person**al**   fame / fam**ous**   nutrient / nutri**tious**

The examples show that a suffix can often help you figure out a word's part of speech.

1 Find and underline the noun forms of the following verbs in the text "Life Expectancy." Then write each noun next to the appropriate verb below.

Verb	Noun Form		Verb	Noun Form	
1 operate	_____	(par. 2)	**5** improve	_____	(par. 3)
2 sanitize	_____	(par. 2)	**6** transport	_____	(par. 5)
3 connect	_____	(par. 3)	**7** refrigerate	_____	(par. 5)
4 prevent	_____	(par. 3)	**8** manage	_____	(par. 6)

2 Read the list of words below. Based on the suffix, decide if each word is a noun (*n.*), or an adjective (*adj.*) and write the correct abbreviation in the blank.

1 personal _____   **4** nutritious _____

2 storage _____   **5** medical _____

3 nutrition _____   **6** environment _____

3 Decide if each sentence below is missing a noun or an adjective, and write *n.* or *adj.* in the blank. Then circle the correct word to complete each sentence.

_____ **1** Pollution has caused many (environment / environmental) problems on Earth.

_____ **2** Good (nutritious / nutrition) can help you live a healthy and long life.

_____ **3** A medical history form asks you for your (personal / personalization) information.

_____ **4** Recycling things is one way to help the (environmental / environment).

_____ **5** The common cold is not a serious (medical / medication) problem.

4 Choose one noun, one adjective, and one verb from steps 1–3. On a separate piece of paper, write three sentences, that is, one sentence for each word you chose.

Task 4   LANGUAGE FOCUS: ADVERBS OF MANNER

An **adverb** is a part of speech that modifies (gives more information about) a verb, an adjective, or another adverb. One type of adverb is an **adverb of manner.** It answers the question *How?*, and it describes the manner, or the way, that someone does something or that something happens.

The doctor washed her hands **carefully.** (How did she wash her hands?)

- Adverbs of manner usually end in *-ly*. They are often formed by adding *-ly* to an adjective (*careful* ➔ *carefully*).

- Be careful! Not all words that end in *-ly* are adverbs. For example, *lonely*, *friendly*, and *healthy* are adjectives, not adverbs. There are also adverbs of manner that do not end in *-ly*, such as *well* and *straight*.

- An adverb of manner often comes after the verb. It never comes between a verb and its object.

CORRECT: He exercises **regularly.**
CORRECT: He lifts weights **regularly.**

INCORRECT: He lifts regularly weights.

1 Read the following sentences, and underline the adverbs of manner in each one.

1 A lack of sanitation causes diseases to spread quickly.

2 Improvements in sanitation helped life expectancy to rise rapidly.

3 Thanks to ships and planes, we can easily transport food long distances.

4 Many centenarians exercise regularly.

2 On a separate piece of paper, rewrite the sentences below. Add an appropriate adverb to each one. You can choose from the adverbs in the box or use your own.

carefully	carelessly	happily	kindly	quickly	quietly	slowly

1 The student conducted the experiment.

2 The doctor talked to the patient.

3 The scientist cleaned the microscope.

4 The researcher walked into the room.

Task 5 UNDERSTANDING A BAR GRAPH

Textbooks often use bar graphs to show statistics. This makes the information easy to read and understand.

1 Look back at Figure 9.1 on page 186. You can also express the data in this bar graph in words. For example:

There were almost 80,000 centenarians in the United States in 2007–2008.

Write two more sentences about the data in Figure 9.1.

1 _____

2 _____

2 Reread paragraph 1 of the text "Life Expectancy." On a separate piece of paper, make a bar graph that compares life expectancy in 1150 (medieval times), 1900, and 2008.

3 Survey your classmates. You can use one of the questions below, or ask your own question about life expectancy.

• What do you think life expectancy in the world will be in 2100?
• Do you know any centenarians?
• Do you think you will live to be a centenarian?

4 Make a bar graph to show the results of your survey. Give the graph a title and write one or two sentences about the data. Present your graph and your sentences to the class.

Task 6 WRITING AN EXPLANATION

For some writing assignments, you will have to explain why something happened. For example, in science classes, you may need to explain why an earthquake occurs, why people have heart attacks, or why an animal species becomes extinct. When you have to write only a short answer, such as one paragraph, it is usually enough to state just two or three reasons and to support each reason with at least one fact or example.

1 Read the following paragraph and answer the questions below with a partner.

There are two reasons why exercise helps people live longer and healthier lives. One reason is that regular exercise can help prevent many diseases. For example, if you exercise, you reduce your risk of developing high blood pressure. You are also less likely to get some types of cancer. The other reason is that exercise makes the heart and lungs stronger. People who have strong hearts and lungs usually have fewer health problems. In addition, they usually recover from sickness faster. For these reasons, doctors agree that exercise can lead to a longer, healthier life.

1 Why does exercise help people live longer and healthier lives?
2 Find and underline the transition words that introduce each reason.

2 Reread the text "Life Expectancy," and find the reasons life expectancy has increased. How many did you find?

3 Highlight the reasons and the facts or examples that support each one.

4 Now write a paragraph that explains why life expectancy has increased in recent years. Remember to include a topic sentence, at least one sentence to support each reason, and a concluding sentence.

Preparing to read

BUILDING VOCABULARY: PREVIEWING KEY WORDS

Read the following paragraph and discuss the questions below in a small group or as a class.

> In the past, many people became ill from influenza, pneumonia, smallpox, measles, and polio. Some people even died from these diseases. However, in the twentieth century, scientists developed antibiotics, such as penicillin, to help sick people get better. They also developed vaccines, which can prevent certain diseases.

1 What are the names of some other diseases?
2 What do you think antibiotics and vaccines are?
3 What are some other things that can help sick people get better?

PREVIEWING KEY PARTS OF A TEXT

1 Preview the title, the headings, and the photographs of the text on pages 193–194 to get a general idea of what it is about. Read the introduction (par. 1) and the first sentence of the other paragraphs. Then answer the following questions:

1 What is the text about? _____

2 What three advances in the field of medicine does the text discuss?

_____ _____ _____

2 Based on your preview of the text, write *T* (true) or *F* (false) next to each of the following sentences.

_____ 1 Antibiotics are dangerous.
_____ 2 Antibiotics were very important during wartime.
_____ 3 Vaccines can help people stay healthy.
_____ 4 Organ transplants are a type of vaccine.
_____ 5 Organ transplants can help people stay alive for a long time.

Now read

Now read the text "Advances in the Field of Medicine." When you finish, turn to the tasks on page 195.

2 ADVANCES IN THE FIELD OF MEDICINE

Today, a fall from a tree, a deep cut from a knife, or exposure to the influenza (flu) virus often results in a trip to the doctor or the hospital. In earlier times, however, any of these experiences might have caused death. Since the mid-twentieth century, medical advances, including the development of antibiotics, vaccines, and new surgical techniques have helped save lives.

1

Antibiotics

Injuries and illness can cause infections. In the past, these infections killed many people. For example, over 20 million people died in the 1918 flu **epidemic**. Many of those people died from pneumonia, an infection of the lungs, caused by the flu. In the twentieth century, doctors and scientists developed a new type of medicine, the antibiotic. One of the most important antibiotics was penicillin, which was first widely used during World War II. When doctors treated pneumonia with penicillin, the number of deaths from this infection decreased dramatically. Now doctors use penicillin and other antibiotics to treat a variety of infections, so that fewer people die from infections today.

2

epidemic
the appearance of a disease in a large number of people at the same time

Dr. Alexander Fleming, the discoverer of penicillin

Vaccines

The development of vaccines has also helped people live longer and healthier lives. Vaccines are medicines that prevent people from catching certain diseases, such as smallpox, measles, and influenza. Today, vaccines provide very effective protection from illness. One good example is smallpox, which was a very serious disease in almost every part of the world. Millions of people died in smallpox epidemics. However, there have not been any cases of smallpox since 1977 because of a global vaccination program that started in the 1950s. Other diseases, such as influenza, polio, and measles, still exist, but today fewer people get sick and die from them because of vaccines.

3

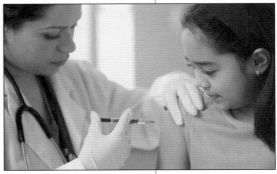

A doctor gives a vaccination.

Developments in surgery

Another reason people are living longer today is the development of new techniques in surgery. A good example is surgery to remove a cancerous tumor. In the past, most people could not survive for a long time with this kind of tumor. Today, many people are able to live long and healthy lives because surgery can get rid of the cancer.

4

Organ transplants have also helped people live longer. For example, in the past, people usually died when their hearts failed. Today, they might receive a heart transplant and live for many more years. Similarly, doctors are now able to perform lung, kidney, and liver transplants.

It is true that antibiotics, vaccines, and developments in surgery have helped many people be healthier and live longer. However, a large number of people in the world still die from preventable diseases. For example, in 2002, more than 2 million people died from diseases that a vaccine could have prevented. Many of those people lived in places where basic medical care is not available. Others could not afford to see a doctor. If good, affordable medical care was available everywhere in the world, it would be possible for even more people to enjoy healthier, longer lives.

Mayo Clinic

William Worrall Mayo, a young Englishman, sailed to the United States in 1846. He became a doctor, and he opened a small office in the farmland of Rochester, Minnesota. Together with his two sons, William and Charles, Mayo built his practice into a small hospital. This was the beginning of Mayo Clinic. The Mayos believed that doctors should learn from each other and work together as a team to give patients the best possible care. They traveled across the country and around the world to learn more about medicine, and they invited the doctors they met to study and lecture at their hospital.

Over the years, Mayo Clinic grew. Today, it is famous worldwide for its research, its use of new surgical techniques, and its excellent care of patients. The staff also wants its patients to feel relaxed. One patient described her visit in this way: "There are displays of beautiful, original art throughout the building. Waiting areas have computer terminals with Internet access, games, and puzzles. Examination rooms have comfortable sofas and chairs. Every staff member was kind, helpful, and extremely knowledgeable. It is truly an amazing place."

More than 3,000 doctors and 45,000 medical staff work at Mayo Clinic. It has three locations, in Minnesota, Florida, and Arizona, where more than half a million patients go every year for treatment.

Statue of the Mayo brothers at
Mayo Clinic in Rochester, Minnesota

After you read

Task 1 TEST TAKING: ANSWERING A VARIETY OF TEST QUESTIONS

Tests and quizzes often consist of a variety of questions instead of just one type. Practicing a mix of questions, such as multiple choice, true/false, and short answer, will make test taking easier.

Answer the questions below, based on information in the text "Advances in the Field of Medicine." When you finish, compare your answers with a partner's.

1 Mark each of the following sentences either *T* (true) or *F* (false):

_____ 1. Surgery is the only reason that life expectancy has increased recently.

_____ 2. Penicillin is a type of antibiotic.

_____ 3. Vaccines can prevent diseases.

_____ 4. Heart transplants can save lives.

_____ 5. Everyone can get affordable medical care when they need it.

2 Circle the best answer for each of the following questions:

1. Which one of the following is not a medical advance?
   a. vaccines
   b. epidemic
   c. organ transplants
   d. antibiotics

2. How many people died in the 1918 flu epidemic?
   a. more than 2,000
   b. more than 20,000
   c. more than 2,000,000
   d. more than 20,000,000

3. Which one of the following is a medicine?
   a. measles
   b. influenza
   c. penicillin
   d. polio

4. Which disease does not make people sick these days?
   a. smallpox
   b. measles
   c. polio
   d. influenza

5. If a person's _____ stops working, an organ transplant may help the person.
   a. body
   b. kidney
   c. brain
   d. skeleton

6. Which one of the following sentences is true?

   a. Everyone who wants vaccines can get them.

   b. Everyone can see a doctor if they want to.

   c. Some people cannot get affordable medical care when they need it.

   d. Some people still die from smallpox today because they do not see a doctor.

3 Answer each of the following questions in one or two sentences. Use your own words. Do not copy sentences from the text.

1. Explain at least one similarity and one difference between antibiotics and vaccines.

   _____

   _____

2. What is an organ transplant?

   _____

   _____

3. Why are some people not able to get good medical care when they need it?

   _____

   _____

Task 2   BUILDING VOCABULARY: USING KEY WORDS

Using key words that you have read in a text will help you understand and remember them.

Complete each of the following questions with a key word from the text "Advances in the Field of Medicine."

1 If you do not want to get the measles, your doctor will give you
a _____.

2 If your heart fails, your doctor might recommend a _____.

3 If a disease is very widespread, it is called an _____.

4 If you cut your hand and get an infection, your doctor might give you
an _____.

5 If you have a cancerous tumor, your doctor might remove it
with _____.

Task 3 LANGUAGE FOCUS: TIME EXPRESSIONS AND VERB TENSES

Within a text and even within a paragraph, writers often switch back and forth between past, present, and future time. Verb tenses and time expressions (*in the past, today, now, in the future*) as well as specific historical events or dates, can help you follow the changes in time.

1 Read the following paragraph, which is based on the text "Advances in the Field of Medicine." Circle the time expressions, and underline the verbs that occur with them.

> In the past, diseases killed millions of people. More than 20 million people in Asia, Africa, North America, and Europe died in the 1918 flu epidemic. However, far fewer people died in the flu epidemics of 1957 and 1968. This was mainly because of the development of antibiotics and vaccines. Today, doctors use antibiotics and vaccines to treat and prevent many illnesses. Doctors hope that in the future they will make more progress in the fight against diseases such as cancer and AIDS.

2 Look back at the text "Advances in the Field of Medicine." Circle the time expressions and underline the verbs that occur with them.

3 Read the paragraph below. There are four mistakes in either time expressions or verb tenses. Find the mistakes and correct them. Then compare your answers with a partner's.

> In the twentieth century, polio is one of the most terrible childhood diseases. Each year, polio struck thousands of people, most of them children, and made some of them unable to walk. In the 1950s, a polio vaccine will be developed. In the past, most of the world's people do not get this disease. However, in a few countries, there are still people who suffer from polio. In the future, doctors hope that polio, like smallpox, disappeared completely.

4 On a separate piece of paper, complete the sentences below. Be sure to use an appropriate verb tense with each time expression.

1 Five years ago, I . . .
Today . . .
In 10 years, I think I . . .

2 In the past, my home . . .
These days, . . .
In the future, I think I . . .

Task 4 NOTE TAKING: CHOOSING A TECHNIQUE THAT WORKS FOR YOU

People usually have their own ways of taking notes about the main ideas and important details of a text. If you choose a technique that works well for you, your notes will help you remember and review the information effectively.

Imagine you are going to have a quiz on paragraphs 2–4 of the text "Advances in the Field of Medicine." To help you review the material, follow the steps below.

1| Reread paragraphs 2–5 of the text. Highlight the main ideas and important details.

2| On a separate piece of paper, either take notes or outline the main ideas and important details and examples. (Review the note-taking tasks on pages 173 and 180, if necessary.)

3| Work in a group of three students. Choose one of the paragraphs you read in step 1, and write two to four questions about it. (Each student should choose a different paragraph). Then try to answer each other's questions, using only your notes or your outline.

Task 5 THINKING CRITICALLY ABOUT THE TOPIC

Discuss the following questions in a small group or as a class.

1| Which improvement do you think is most important for helping people live longer, healthier lives today? Explain your answer.

- antibiotics
- better nutrition
- better sanitation
- vaccines
- lifestyle changes for better health
- better surgical techniques

2| Do doctors often use antibiotics and vaccines where you live? Were these medicines common in places where you have lived in the past? What are some advantages and disadvantages of these medicines?

3| Is surgery common where you live or in places where you have lived? What are some advantages and disadvantages of surgery?

4| What do you think governments, organizations, and individuals could do to make sure everyone in the world gets affordable medical care when they need it?

Task 6   UNDERSTANDING CAUSE AND EFFECT

Academic texts often discuss why something happens (reasons or causes), and what happens as a result (effects). For example, in a science text, you may read about the causes and effects of earthquakes, global warming, or heart attacks.

The following sentences show examples of words and phrases that signal cause and effect:

cause

effect

- The flu can **cause**   fever, headaches, tiredness, and a sore throat.

cause

effect

- The development of antibiotics   is   **one reason** people live longer today.

cause

effect

- A heart transplant   **results in**   a new heart for a person with heart problems.

Sometimes the cause and the effect can be in reverse order.

effect

cause

- Today, fewer people die from measles   **because**   they get vaccinated.
- Today, fewer people die from measles   **because of**   vaccines.

1 Read the sentences below. In each sentence, underline the cause once and the effect twice.

1 Some people do not get vaccines because they are too expensive.

2 Infections can cause death.

3 Another reason many people died in the twentieth century was smallpox epidemics.

4 Advances in the medical field often result in more people living longer.

2 Read the following paragraph and discuss the questions below.

> There are three major reasons for heart failure. First, a person's heart may fail because of bad habits, such as smoking, eating fatty foods, and not exercising. Viruses can also cause heart failure. For example, the coxsackie virus can damage the heart muscle and cause it to fail. In addition, heart problems that a person is born with can result in heart failure. Doctors are studying these three causes because they want to improve the treatment of their patients.

1 What is the main idea of the paragraph?

2 Does this paragraph mainly discuss causes or effects?

3 How many causes does the writer discuss? What are they?

4 Underline all the words and phrases that signal cause and effect.

Preparing to read

THINKING ABOUT THE TOPIC BEFORE YOU READ

Discuss the following questions in a small group or as a class:

1 Do you think the natural world has changed in the past 100 years? If so, do you think these changes have been positive or negative? Explain your answer.

2 What do you think the natural world will be like in 100 years?

3 What are some things that people are doing to protect the natural world?

INCREASING YOUR READING SPEED

1 Review the strategies for increasing your reading speed on page 66.

2 Write your starting time. Then read the text "Seeking Balance in the Natural World," using the speed-reading strategies.

Starting time: _____

3 Fill in the time you finished.

Finishing time: _____

Then calculate your reading speed:
Number of words in the text (841) ÷
Number of minutes it took you to
read the text = your reading speed

Reading speed: _____

Your goal should be about 80–100 words per minute.

4 Check your reading comprehension. Circle the correct answers to complete the sentences below. Do not look back at the text.

1 Balance in the natural world is (good / bad / neither good nor bad).

2 There are (the same number of / more / fewer) people in the world today than 100 years ago.

3 (Pollution / Loss of forests / The destruction of homes) kills millions of people each year.

4 People's actions to protect the natural world have (helped / hurt / had no effect).

Now read

Now read the text "Seeking Balance in the Natural World" again. Then check your answers to step 4 above. When you finish, turn to the tasks on page 203.

3 SEEKING BALANCE IN THE NATURAL WORLD

Life in the natural world includes a wide variety of plants and animals. The health of our natural world depends on keeping this **biodiversity** in balance. This means that we must make sure that species of plants and animals have what they need to survive: a place to live, a comfortable climate, nutritious food, clean water, and breathable air.

1

biodiversity
the great variety of living organisms and their habitats on Earth

Today, people are living longer, and as a result, there are more people on Earth than ever before. The population increase has been rapid. In 1804, there were 1 billion people; less than 200 years later, in 1974, there were 4 billion people; and in 2008, there were more than 6.5 billion people on our planet. As we try to satisfy the needs of this growing population, we are also harming the balance in the natural world.

2

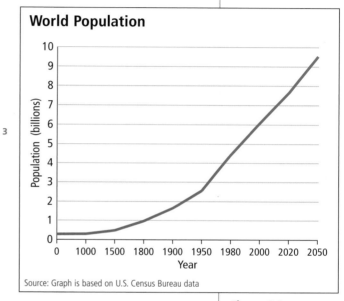

World Population

Source: Graph is based on U.S. Census Bureau data

Figure 9.2

A world out of balance

One of the most serious problems we face is water pollution. With more people on Earth, there is more waste material. For many years, people used to get rid of waste and garbage by dumping it into the water. As a result, much of the water in our oceans, rivers, lakes, and ground is polluted, and the supply of clean drinking water has decreased. In fact, almost 1.5 billion people on our planet do not have safe drinking water, and at least 5 million people die each year from waterborne diseases. Many organisms that were living in polluted waters, such as fish and seals, have also died.

3

Air pollution is another major problem. As the population grows, so does the need for more homes, cars, and manufactured products. Heating homes, driving cars, and manufacturing products produce carbon dioxide and other polluting gases, such as carbon monoxide and sulfur dioxide. Air pollution causes more than 2 million deaths each year. The increased amount of polluting gases also changes the balance of gases in the atmosphere. This leads to global warming and the environmental problems it causes.

4

In order to build more homes and grow more food, people have destroyed the natural habitats of many plants and animals. In fact, approximately half of the forests that once covered Earth are now gone. When plants and animals lose their homes, they often become extinct. Just two examples are the Carolina parakeet and the Javan tiger. There are also many species that are nearly extinct, such as the Philippine eagle and the Sumatran tiger. Other species in danger include elephants, pandas, mountain gorillas, spotted owls and tropical orchids. When one

5

species becomes extinct, other species that depend on that species suffer, and they may also die out. For example, based on a recent study, a group of scientists made this prediction: If the 6,279 plants now on the endangered list became extinct, 4,672 species of beetles and 136 types of butterflies would also become extinct. There are important interconnections among all species of plants and animals, and they depend on each other for survival.

Restoring balance

We now have a chance to restore some of the balance in our natural world before it is too late. Today, many countries have both government agencies and private organizations that work to protect the environment. Environmental protection is also becoming a popular topic in schools, at international conferences, in newspapers, and in daily conversations. More and more people are learning about the damage to the natural world, and many are taking action to improve the situation. 6

People are trying to protect nature in various ways. Some people are cleaning up the water and the air by building wind energy farms, water treatment centers, and electric cars. Others are trying to restore damaged habitats, grow more trees, and preserve, or save, endangered plants and animals. For example, in the 1970s, the bald eagle and the American peregrine falcon were both endangered. The United States government made laws to try to protect the birds. As a result, these birds are not endangered anymore, and they are living successfully in their natural habitats. 7

Bald eagle

Even smaller steps can help. In Asia, for example, people now bring their own reusable chopsticks when they go out to eat, instead of using the disposable wooden ones in restaurants. This small act saves thousands of trees each year. In Lebanon, where deforestation is a big problem, an organization of young people has planted 250,000 cedar trees in the past 10 years. In Brazil, more than 12,000 students took classes in environmental studies. Then they worked in companies, teaching the employees about environmental issues, such as water conservation and waste collection. They are helping to preserve the Brazilian savannah (grasslands), which covers 24 percent of the country. In cities across the United States, people are planting rooftop gardens in order to reduce air pollution and improve air quality. 8

Volunteers pick up waste on a beach.

The challenges of our environmental problems can sometimes seem overwhelming. However, there is a lot we can do, as countries, as communities, and as individuals, to help the natural world. The future of our planet demands that we act with courage, intelligence, creativity, and cooperation. Many people believe that, through our efforts, we can, indeed, save our planet. 9

After you read

Task 1 ASKING FOR CLARIFICATION

Review the strategies for asking for clarification on page 144. Then do the following activities:

1| Find words and ideas in the text "Seeking Balance in the Natural World" and Figure 9.2 that you would like to clarify. Then take turns with a partner, asking and answering clarification questions.

2| Are there any words or ideas that you still do not understand clearly? If so, choose one of them, and ask your teacher a question to clarify the meaning.

Task 2 NOTE TAKING: CHOOSING A TECHNIQUE THAT WORKS FOR YOU

1| Work with a partner. Divide the text "Seeking Balance in the Natural World" between you: paragraphs 1–5 and paragraphs 6–9. Reread your half of the text and highlight the main ideas and important details.

2| On a separate piece of paper, either take notes or outline the main ideas and important details and examples for your half of the text.

3| Then explain your half of the text to your partner. Use your notes or outline for guidance.

Task 3 TEST TAKING: WRITING YOUR OWN TEST QUESTIONS

> To help you prepare for a test or quiz on a text, it is often useful to write your own test questions. This is an effective way to review the main ideas and important details.

1| Work with your partner from task 2. Write eight to ten test questions that cover the whole text "Seeking Balance in the Natural World." Include true/false, multiple choice, and short-answer questions. Review the test-taking tasks on pages 21, 35, and 61, if necessary.

2| Exchange tests with another group and take each other's test. Then look back at the text to check your answers.

Task 4 LANGUAGE FOCUS: INFINITIVES

> When two verbs appear together, the second verb is sometimes in the
> infinitive form (*to* + verb).
>
> verb 1   verb 2 (infinitive)
> As we try   to satisfy human needs, we often harm the natural world.

1| In paragraph 7 of the text, underline the examples of verbs in infinitive form.

2| Complete the following sentences based on information in the text. Use infinitive
forms correctly.

1 In the twentieth century, the population began to _____.

2 The more people there are on Earth, the more _____ they need
to _____.

3 Some people are trying _____ in order to preserve
the natural world.

4 In order to protect nature, more people should try _____
_____.

5 To protect our planet, I want _____.

Task 5 BUILDING VOCABULARY: SYNONYMS AND ANTONYMS

1| Match the words in the column on the left with their synonyms (words with similar
meaning) on the right.

_____ **1** grow	**a** home
_____ **2** major	**b** increase
_____ **3** damage	**c** harm
_____ **4** habitat	**d** save
_____ **5** preserve	**e** big

2| Match the words in the column on the left with their antonyms (opposites) on
the right.

_____ **1** reusable	**a** polluted
_____ **2** increase	**b** save
_____ **3** help	**c** disposable
_____ **4** destroy	**d** harm
_____ **5** clean	**e** reduce

Task 6 THINKING CRITICALLY ABOUT THE TOPIC

Discuss the following questions in a small group:

1 What do you think is the biggest problem facing the natural world today?

2 What do you think governments should do to protect the environment?

3 What do you do to help protect the planet? What is one more thing you could do?

Task 7 CONDUCTING A SURVEY

1 Survey at least five people. You can use one of the questions below or ask your own question about the natural world.

- What do you think is the most serious environmental issue today?
- What do you think is the most important thing people can do to protect nature?
- Do you think you are doing enough to protect the natural world?
- Do you think we will be successful in saving the natural world?

2 Make a bar graph or a pie chart to show the results of your survey. (Review the information about bar graphs on pages 184 and 190, and pie charts on page 17, if necessary.) Give the graph or chart a title, and write a few sentences that explain the information. Present your graph or chart and your sentences to the class.

Task 8 WRITING ABOUT CAUSE AND EFFECT

1 Review the signals of cause and effect in "Understanding Cause and Effect" on page 199.

2 Look back at the text "Seeking Balance in the Natural World." Circle the words and phrases that signal cause and effect. Label the causes (*C*) and the effects (*E*).

3 Study these additional ways to show cause and effect.

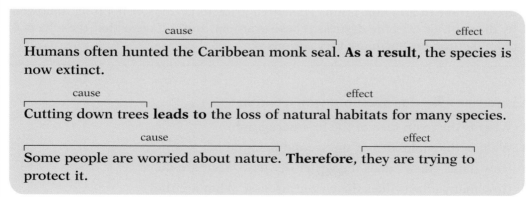

cause / effect
Humans often hunted the Caribbean monk seal. As a result, the species is now extinct.

cause / effect
Cutting down trees leads to the loss of natural habitats for many species.

cause / effect
Some people are worried about nature. Therefore, they are trying to protect it.

4 The word *deforestation* means "destroying forests by cutting down trees." In a small group, brainstorm two causes and two effects of deforestation.

Causes of deforestation	Effects of deforestation
1	1
2	2

5 Write two sentences: one sentence about the cause of deforestation and one sentence about the effect.

1 _____

2 _____

6 Read the following text about deforestation. Notice that one paragraph focuses on causes of deforestation, and the other paragraph focuses on effects.

There are several causes of deforestation in the world today. All of the causes are related to the growing population of the world. One major cause is construction. People need more and more wood to build homes and furniture. Therefore, they are cutting down more trees. Another reason for deforestation is the need for new land to grow food. In addition, people need fuel. Many people are using trees as firewood for cooking and heating. For these reasons, deforestation continues on our planet.

Our planet suffers from deforestation in important ways. First, cutting down forests causes a decrease in biodiversity. In fact, many species are now endangered or extinct because of deforestation. Cutting down trees can also result in environmental problems. When forests are cut down, they can no longer absorb (take in and hold) rain. This often leads to periods of flooding, followed by drought, or extreme dryness. These examples make it clear that the effects of deforestation on Earth are very serious.

7 Answer the following questions with a partner:

1 What is the main idea of the first paragraph?

2 What is the main idea of the second paragraph?

3 How many causes does the writer discuss? What are they?

4 How many effects does the writer discuss? What are they?

5 Underline all the words and phrases that signal cause and effect.

Chapter 9   Writing Assignment

Write two paragraphs about the causes and effects of one problem facing our world today. For example, you could write about overpopulation, problems with health care, endangered species, climate change, or the destruction of natural habitats. Use information from this chapter and other chapters in this book, if appropriate. Find some additional information in the library or on the Internet. Follow the steps and the guidelines below.

1 Choose a problem and find some information about it. Take notes on what you find.

2 Discuss what you learned with a partner or in a small group.

3 Then, on your own, brainstorm about the causes and effects of the problem. Use a chart like the one on page 206 to organize your ideas.

4 Choose two or three causes and two or three effects that you want to include in your writing.

5 Now write the first draft of the paragraphs.

> **Guidelines**
> - Write about causes in the first paragraph and effects in the second paragraph.
> - For each paragraph, include a topic sentence, at least one supporting sentence for each cause and each effect, and a concluding sentence.
> - Include any relevant vocabulary and information from this chapter.
> - Use words and phrases that signal cause and effect where appropriate.
> - Include some time expressions and appropriate verb tenses (see the Language Focus task, page 197).
> - Give your work a title.

6 When you finish writing, exchange paragraphs with a partner and read each other's work. Then discuss the following questions about both pieces of work:

   1 Which information in your partner's paragraphs do you think is the most interesting?

   2 Does your partner's writing have correct form and structure?

   3 Does it include some expressions of cause and effect?

   4 Are all the sentences relevant to the topic?

   5 Are the ideas presented in a logical order?

7 Think about any changes to your paragraphs that would improve them. Then write a second draft.

Weights and Measures

The metric system is the system of measurement that all scientists use. It is also used by people in most countries of the world. In the United States, most non-scientists use the U.S. system. Some Web sites offer a free converter that you can use to convert measurements from one system to the other.

EXAMPLES OF THE METRIC SYSTEM AND ITS EQUIVALENTS IN THE U.S. SYSTEM

The metric system is based on the number 10, and it uses different prefixes for smaller and larger units. For example, a kilometer is 1,000 meters, a centimeter is one-hundredth of a meter (.01 meter), and a millimeter is one-thousandth of a meter (.001 meter).

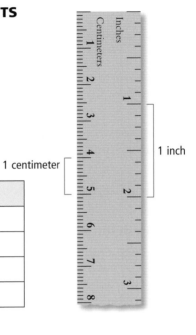

1 centimeter

1 inch

Units of length

Metric system		U.S. system
1 millimeter (mm)		= 0.03937 inch
10 mm	= 1 centimeter (cm)	= 0.3937 inch
100 cm	= 1 meter (m)	= 39.37 inches
1000 m	= 1 kilometer (km)	= 0.6214 mile

Units of weight

Metric system		U.S. system
1 milligram (mg)		= 0.000035 ounce
1000 mg	= 1 gram (g)	= 0.035 ounce
1000 g	= 1 kilogram (kg)	= 2.205 pounds
1000 kg	= 1 metric ton	= 2,205 pounds

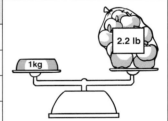

Units of liquid volume

Metric system		U.S. system
1 milliliter (ml)		= 0.03 fluid ounces
1000 ml	= 1 liter (l)	= 33.81 fluid ounces
3.785 liters		= 1 gallon

1 liter   1 gallon

EXAMPLES OF THE U.S. SYSTEM AND ITS EQUIVALENTS IN THE METRIC SYSTEM

Units of length

U.S. system		Metric system
1 inch (in)		= 2.54 centimeters
12 in	= 1 foot (ft)	= 0.3048 meters
3 ft	= 1 yard (yd)	= 0.9144 meters
1760 yd (5,280 ft)	= 1 mile (mi)	= 1.609 kilometers

Units of weight

U.S. system		Metric system
1 ounce (oz)		= 28.35 grams
16 oz	= 1 pound (lb)	= 0.4536 kilograms
2,000 lb	= 1 ton	= 907.18 kilograms

Units of liquid volume

U.S. system		Metric system
1 fluid ounce (fl oz)	= 0.007813 gallons (gal)	= 29.57 milliliters
32 fl oz	= 0.25 gal = 1 quart (qt)	= 0.9464 liters
128 fl oz	= 1 gal	= 3.785 liters

Temperature Scales

Scientists and most countries in the world use the Celsius, or centigrade, scale (°C) to measure temperature. In the United States, most people use the Fahrenheit scale (°F).

To convert temperatures from one scale to the other, use these formulas:

degrees Fahrenheit = (°Celsius × 1.8) + 32
degrees Celsius = (°Fahrenheit − 32) × 0.55

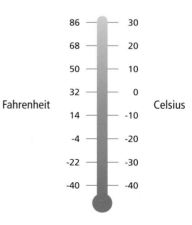

Fahrenheit   Celsius

Map of the World

Arctic Ocean

Greenland

Alaska
U.S.

Iceland

Norway

United Kingdom

Denmark

Ireland

Netherlands

Belgium

Switzerland

France

Canada

Atlantic Ocean

Portugal

Spain

Tunisia

Morocco

Algeria

United States

Western Sahara

Mauritania

Mali

Niger

Senegal

Gambia

Hawaiian Islands
U.S.

Mexico

Cuba

Dominican
Republic

Belize

Jamaica

Puerto Rico

Guinea-Bissau

Guinea

Burkina Faso

Guatemala

Honduras

Haiti

Sierra Leone

Ghana

Nigeria

El Salvador

Nicaragua

Liberia

Togo

Costa Rica

Venezuela

Suriname

Côte d'Ivoire

Panama

French Guiana

Colombia

Guyana

Galapagos
Islands

Ecuador

Pacific Ocean

Peru

Brazil

Bolivia

Paraguay

Chile

Uruguay

Argentina

N

W   E

S

Southern Ocean

References

Barrett, Norman S. *Rivers and Lakes*. New York: Franklin Watts Ltd., 1989.

Berger, Gilda. *The Human Body*. New York: Doubleday Books for Young Readers, 1989.

Biggs, A., L. Daniel, E. Orttleb., et al. *Life Science*. New York: McGraw-Hill Companies, Inc., 2005.

Bramwell, Martin. *Oceans*. New York: Franklin Watts, Inc., 1984.

Bramwell, Martin. *Rivers and Lakes*. New York: Franklin Watts, Inc., 1986.

Collins, Tim, and Mary Jane Maples. *Gateway to Science: Vocabulary and Concepts*. Boston: Thomson Heinle, 2008.

Farndon, John. *Dictionary of the Earth*. New York: DK Publishing, 1994.

Graun, Ken, and Thomas J. Bopp. *Our Earth and the Solar System*. Tucson, AZ: Ken Press, 2000.

Hamilton, John. *Tsunamis (Nature's Fury)*. Edina, MN: ABDO & Daughters, 2006.

Harris, Nicholas, Joanna Turner, and Claire Aston, eds. *Planet Earth*. Farmington Hills, MI: Gales Cengage Learning, 2000.

Haslam, Andrew, and Barbara Taylor. *Oceans*. Chicago: World Book, Inc., 1997.

Hess, F. S., G. Kunze, S. Leslie, et al. *Earth Science: Geology, the Environment, and the Universe*. Columbus, OH: The McGraw-Hill Companies, Inc., 2005.

Kerrod, Robin. *Planet Earth*. Minneapolis: Lerner Publications Company, 2000.

Lyons, Walter A. *The Handy Weather Answer Book*. Detroit: Gale Research, 1997.

McGraw-Hill Concise Encyclopedia of Earth Science, 5th ed., 2005.

Newquist, Harvey P. *The Great Brain Book: An Inside Look at the Inside of Your Head*. New York: Scholastic, Inc, 2005.

Podesto, Martine, Ed. *Scholastic Atlas of Earth*. Montreal: QA International, 2004.

Scientific American Science Desk Reference. New York: John Wiley, 1999.

Sills, Alan D. *Earth Science the Easy Way*. Hauppage, NY: Barron's Educational Series, 2003.

Simon, Seymour. *The Brain: Our Nervous System*. New York: William Morrow and Company, Inc., 1997.

Smith, David. *The Water Cycle*. New York: Thomson Learning, 1993.

Snedden, Robert, and Chris Fairclough. *Rocks and Soil (Science Projects)*. Austin, Tex: Steck-Vaughn Company, 1999.

Strahler, Arthur N. *Introduction to Physical Geography*. 2nd ed. New York: John Wiley, 1970.

Symes, R. F., and the staff of the Natural History Museum, London. *Eyewitness: Rocks & Minerals*. New York: DK Publishing, Inc., 2004.

Symes, R. F. and R. R. Harding. *Eyewitness: Crystal & Gem*. New York: DK Publishing, Inc., 2004.

Tarbuck, Edward J., and Frederick K. Lutgens. *Earth Science*. 6th ed. New York: Macmillan, 1991.

Vekteris, Donna. *Scholastic Atlas of Oceans*. New York: Scholastic, Inc, 2004.

Vogel, Carole G. *Savage Waters*. New York: Franklin Watts, Inc., 2003.

Walker, Richard. *The Human Body*. Boston: Kingfisher, 2006.

Ward, Brian R. *The Skeleton and Movement*. New York: Franklin Watts, Inc., 1981.

York, Penelope. *Earth*. London: DK Publishing, 2002.

Credits

PHOTOGRAPHIC AND ILLUSTRATION CREDITS

Cover © Reprinted by permission of the family of Walter Inglis Anderson

1 © Courtesy of Nasa

2 *(left to right)* © Courtesy of Nasa; © Courtesy of Nasa; © istockphoto;

3 © Courtesy of Nasa

5 *(left to right)* © Shutterstock; © Tetra Images/Alamy

6 © Breen/Creators Syndicate

13 © Ron Carboni

14 © HADJ/SIPA/Associated Press

18 © istockphoto

19 *(clockwise from top left)* © istockphoto; © Erik Reis/Alamy; © RF Company/Alamy

20 © J. Adam Huggins/New York Times

22 © Vilma Ortiz-Dillon

28 © John Batten

32 © Phil Degginger/Alamy

38 © Courtesy of USGS

39 © Courtesy of USGS

41 © Courtesy of USGS

47 © istockphoto

48 © istockphoto

49 © istockphoto

51 © Getty Images

52 © Vilma Ortiz-Dillon

59 © Ron Carboni

60 © istockphoto

67 *(top to bottom)* © istockphoto; © Steven J. Kazlowski/Alamy

73 © Courtesy of Nasa

74 © Clipart.com

79 © The Kobal Collection

81 © John Batten

82 © Vilma Ortiz-Dillon

83 © John Batten

87 © Bebeto Matthews/Associated Press

88 © Newscom

91 © Courtesy of the Bishop Museum

93 © Peter Cade/Getty Images

95 © Peter Cade/Getty Images

97 © Courtesy of Nasa

98 © Sakchai Lalit/Associated Press

103 © Ron Carboni

104 © AFP/Getty Images

108 *(clockwise from top left)* © istockphoto; © istockphoto; © istockphoto; © Clipart.com; © Clipart.com; © istockphoto

109 istockphoto

110 *(top to bottom)* © istockphoto; © Vilma Ortiz-Dillon

114 © Vilma Ortiz-Dillon

115 © istockphoto

116 © Shutterstock

117 *(clockwise from top left)* © Fiona McIntosh/age Fotostock © AFP/Getty Images; © Shutterstock

118 © Graham Simmons/Photographers Direct

122 © istockphoto

123 *(top to bottom)* © istockphoto; © Courtesy of Nasa

124 © Jim Reed/Getty Images

129 © Associated Press

131 © Courtesy of Nasa

132 © Photos.com

135 © Courtesy of Nasa

137 © istockphoto

139 © istockphoto

140 © Vilma Ortiz-Dillon

141 © istockphoto

142 *(left to right)* © Dr. Richard Kessel & Dr. Gene Shih/Getty Images; © Phototake Inc./Alamy

147 © istockphoto

148 © D. Hurst/Alamy

150 © John Batten

TEXT CREDITS

Task Index

Many of the tasks in *Academic Encounters: The Natural World* (as well as those in all *Academic Encounters* books) teach academic skills tested on the TOEFL® iBT test.

*Page numbers in **boldface** indicate tasks that are headed by commentary boxes.*